TWICE OVER LIGHTLY

BOOKS BY ERIC NICOL

SENSE AND NONSENSE

THE ROVING I

TWICE OVER LIGHTLY

Twice Over Lightly

ERIC
NICOL

Illustrations by
JAMES SIMPKINS

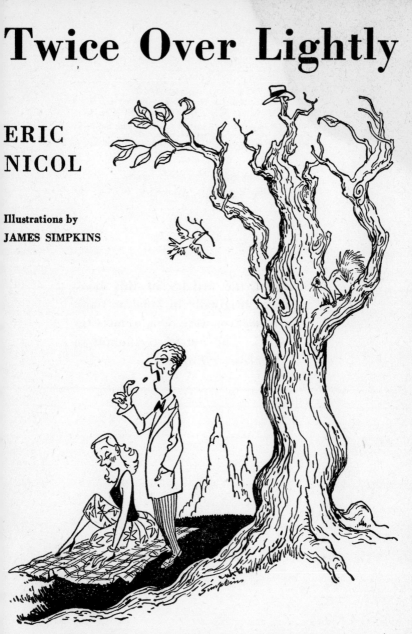

The Ryerson Press ~ Toronto

Published, September, 1953
Second printing, November, 1953

Some of the articles in this book appeared originally in *Maclean's* and *The Beaver,* or were done as talks for the CBC. The rest were columns in *The Vancouver Province.*

PRINTED AND BOUND IN CANADA
BY THE RYERSON PRESS, TORONTO

DEDICATION

This was written for the Money

FORWARD!

THIS is my third collection of short pieces, as good an example as you're likely to find of not knowing when to quit.

The first two collections sold out quickly, thanks to the publisher's printing only 10 copies of each. Most of the copies were sold just before Christmas (about 12 hours before), and the biggest sales were recorded at Vancouver bookstalls, where I was able to encourage sales by personal appearances. The purchaser just had to show me his receipt and I cleaned his turkey for him.

Needless to say, when you've had a couple of books published, and you've acquired a taste for royalties, you get to know quite well some of the people who sell your books — the women clerks particularly. I myself am married to three of them. This is in line with the publisher's encouraging his authors to fraternize with the booksellers, discuss their problems, discover their hobbies, do their laundry—just generally make themselves useful. Anybody can write a book, but it takes talent and tact to have the book displayed to advantage on the book counter.

The best place for your book is on the direct line from the door to the books on sex. (If your book *is* a book on sex you can afford to be practically anywhere, any dark corner, the darker the better.)

Large atlases are a bad thing to be heaped behind, and it is a good idea for your book to stay clear of works by Hemingway, Faulkner and that crowd. When people browse around your book it should be surrounded by literary stubble—books on how to build a drop forge, translations of lesser Greek poets, that sort of thing.

It is also useful to drop around to the book counter about once a week, take from the pile the top, dusty copy of your book, open it and chuckle at it for a few minutes, then slip it under the pile and walk away. I have found that many readers suffer from hayfever and will not pick up a book with dust on the jacket, no matter how much they want to read you. If you have time it is not a bad idea to scatter a little dust on the books around yours. The collectings from a vacuum cleaner, shaken gently in a paper bag with small holes in the bottom, give gratifying results.

Thanks to this sort of imaginative promotion, my books went into a second printing (10 more copies of each). One of them was chosen by the Book of the Month Club. Not the New York one, but the Book of the Month Club in Milkweed, Manitoba. Brunhilda Smith, who runs the lending library there, chooses a book every month, basing her selection on the books her husband, a CNR trainman, finds left on the seats.

It was evident that now nothing could stop me from going ahead. In fact that's what my publisher said when I told them I was preparing a new book. "If you want to go ahead, we can't stop you," they wrote. It was all the encouragement I needed.

But I know that thin volumes of short pieces like

this have stiffer competition these days. Canadians are now writing full-grown books, books with a beginning, a middle, an ending—sometimes all three. The Americans still have all the four-letter words, but several Canadian novelists are down to five letters and are busy replacing descriptions of autumn leaves with fast action involving women.

In the midst of this literary ferment it may be dangerously static to keep offering accumulations of light essays, suitable for the whole family except that the whole family is reading *What Every Ghoul Should Know* or something and doesn't want to be disturbed. I guess it's time I developed. Next year, maybe. This year I want to concentrate on my putting.

—E. N.

Vancouver, 1953.

CONTENTS

Contents

LIST OF ILLUSTRATIONS

xiii

CUCKOO IN KENT

A CUCKOO cooed.

I looked out my window across the lovely fields of Kent bright with morning, and plucked my shaving brush nervously.

The Colonel and his wife, ardent supporters of the white man's burden, had invited me down for the weekend. I knew their niece and they wanted to know how well. The Colonel had put me in a room full of bullets and relics of battle. I had slept restlessly and been awakened by a strange old woman bearing tea whom I assumed to be either "Nanny" or one of Macbeth's witches.

Now I stood in my dressing-gown listening for some sound of other people getting up.

I wasn't sure what time English gentry rose on Sunday mornings. I didn't want to barge off to the bathroom ahead of cue. I coughed and listened for an answering cough. Silence.

Putting a towel around my neck I tiptoed to my door and opened it very carefully. I put my head out the door and looked straight into the eyes of the Colonel. His head was just far enough out his door for me to see that he had a towel around his neck.

"Well, so you're up at last," he said hoarsely.

"Yes, sir." I had been up for a little over an hour, or long enough to have a bellyful of cuckoo.

1

There followed the verbal *pas de deux* of Waving the Other Chap Through to the Bathroom—"You go ahead," "No, no, you." "No, I'll wait, etc."—a ritual as classic as the mating dance of the whooping crane.

I went in first. I was no sooner hacking away at the stubble than I saw the doorknob turning. Perspiring slightly I hacked faster and was soon searching shelves for a styptic pencil. The doorknob resumed its revolutions, with a definite effort being made to pull the door off the bolt. I wondered whether Emily Post had covered this particular situation, whether the incumbent should release the bolt, throwing the exterior party off balance, or merely shout some word of encouragement, or sit tight and trust the hinges.

Having hurriedly brushed the four teeth that showed, I darted back to my room and closed the door, panting.

"Coo-coo!" cooed the cuckoo.

Dressed, I went downstairs to wait for the others. I was idling in the hall when I happened to glance into the dining-room. The others were all there, waiting. They were sitting around the table in pyjamas and dressing-gowns, unwashed, unshaved, but obviously disgruntled because they hadn't been able to get into the bathroom at all.

My impulse was to run upstairs and put my pyjamas back on. A creaking stair gave me away, however, and I was called into the dining-room. I felt awfully small, but they could still see me. They could see I was overdressed for an English Sunday breakfast. My four brushed teeth shone blatantly. In a glade beside my ear a merry brook of blood showed I'd shaved. I couldn't have felt more colonial if I

2

had been wearing ostrich feathers and a bone through my nose.

"Sit down, Canada," said the Colonel, secretly pleased, I thought, with this evidence that the Dominion was not ready for self-government. To demonstrate how cold the toast had become, he took a piece from its rack and broke it. It went off like a pistol shot.

"How did you sleep?" asked the Colonel's wife, leaning forward so that her negligee made me fumble the bran flakes.

"On my stomach," I said. I was flustered.

After that conversation languished while everybody but me read the Sunday papers. I just bled quietly.

And a cuckoo in Kent cooed "Coo-coo!"

HOW TO TAKE A TRAIN

RAILWAY travel is old-fashioned. It's archaic. It's safe. Here's how to take a train.

We'll assume that you've decided to go someplace by rail. Now, these days you can fly almost anywhere that the train goes. This is the Age of Flight. Progress has got you by the short hairs. When you tell your friends that you are going somewhere, the first thing they'll say will be:

"Are you flying?"

This is a question you can't just say "No" to. If you just say "No" and change the subject your friends are liable to think you're afraid to fly. On the other hand, it's useless to try to explain to them this psychic knowledge you have that the airplane is out to get you and the second you set foot inside one it will blow up. Friends never understand that sort of thing. Friends want to think you're an old yellowbelly, like them.

So, as soon as you make up your mind to take the train you should immediately make up some reasons for not taking a plane. Here are a few I've had varying results with:

1. To the question "Are you flying?" reply "No, I'm going by train for a change." *For a change.* There is no need to specify that the train will be a change from riding the streetcar.

4

2. "Have to think about the wife and kids." (Less effective with people who know you're single.)

3. "Want to see the wildflowers." (No good in winter, in fact not much good at all.)

4. "A friend of mine is going by train and I thought it would be fun to go with her." (To be used with caution with lady friends and members of the clergy.)

Now you're ready to slink into the railway station and buy your ticket. (I myself usually buy my train tickets from a travel agency, wearing dark glasses and simulating someone from out of town by asking the way to the station.)

Comes the day of departure. You're all packed, except for the things you've forgotten. Some people believe in taking a number of small pieces of baggage instead of one or two large ones. Then, if they don't find a redcap, they can carry the small pieces to the train themselves by making several round trips. Of course if they do find a redcap the whole scheme is fouled up.

People will be coming to the station to see you off. You can't stop them. They want to make sure you go. After you have shaken hands with everybody and said good-bye and Mother has got a good weep on, the P.A. system announces that your train won't leave for another half-hour.

The experienced train-taker is prepared for this. After the emotional peak of good-byes, and with Mother still snivelling, he knows he can't go back to chatter about hockey scores. He therefore cries:

"My goodness, I can't find my ticket!" at the same time searching his pockets. Soon the entire party is busy scouring the station, retracing steps to the sidewalk, and chasing down the station master. In the excitement one of the children can usually be counted on to get lost, providing the bonus panic of his possibly having wandered into the yard amongst the rails and engines. In this way the half-hour delay passes quickly, and the traveller finds his ticket, in his pocket after all, just in time to wave bye-bye.

Your accommodation on the train may be either day-coach or pullman. If you have a seat in the day-coach, you will want to keep the seat beside you empty so that you can put your feet up there later on. Peeling an orange will discourage many people from sitting beside you, but even more efficient is a hand-kerchief soaked with eucalyptus held to the face as other passengers pass along the aisle. Most people will get as far away from eucalyptus as the length of the train permits.

If you have space in a pullman you must impress the porter right off as a veteran traveller who expects service. When he reaches for your bags, don't wrestle with him. Also don't stand back to allow him to board the train first. Just march right on as though you were going to give him a big tip at the end of the journey.

If you have an upper berth, lose no time showing it who is master. Climb right into it, even though it means stepping more or less indiscriminately on the ladder, the porter's fingers and the face of the occupant of the lower. If you fall out, climb back in before you lose your nerve or your pyjamas or something.

Also, you need have no trouble in removing your trousers in your berth. The essence of the movement is nothing more than natural body rhythm and a sense of timing and a head of teak. If you can dance there is no reason why you cannot get your pants off in a pullman berth.

Once under way about all you have to watch is that you don't strike up a friendship with a young woman just before the dining-car steward comes through the car bonging his gong. (Or, if you are a young woman, make sure you do strike up a friendship just before etc., etc.) The price of a dinner for two in the dining-car these days can cut your trip down by as much as 200 miles.

The best time to make friends on a train is between the last call for dinner and the first call for breakfast. If, for some reason, a man finds himself in female company dangerously close to a meal-time, he can always spring up suddenly, exclaiming:

"By George, I must send that telegram to Uncle Henry," and tool off to the men's smoker. You may have to stay there a while, so always carry an apple.

Getting off the train is the easiest part, provided the train has stopped. Once again you say good-bye, this time to the people you've met on the train. If any of these people are female or elderly with heavy baggage, it is advisable to descend the steps to the platform stiff-legged. This will clear you for carrying your own bags as far as the station, where you can make a run for it.

Bon voyage!

PASSION'S PLAYTHING, FREE

I HAVE had an urgent message from a D. B. Carlton of Toronto.

According to this "flash-o-gram," if I act at once I shall receive FREE with membership "the sensation-packed new best-seller, *The Infinite Woman*." Accompanying the urgent flash-o-gram, which by some contretemps of communication was delivered by our postman, who wasn't even running, is a tinted folder headed: "I'll be your friend—your confidante —but never your bride!" And beside this limited offer pulses the picture of a woman.

Oh, my.

She is voluptuous, that's what she is, this woman. She is lying somewhere in a slinky, strapless gown that obviously wasn't designed just to give greater freedom for ping-pong. She is looking straight at me. Her dark eyes are smoldering, and thanks to the prevailing wind sparks have blown over me and I am now blazing out of control.

This breeze that Mr. Carlton shoots comes from the small print swathing the woman's curves. As soon as my eyes boinged back into their sockets, I read:

"In Lola Montero's lovely body flowed warm Irish blood, spiced with a fiery Spanish strain—but her spirit was completely pagan. While still a child in a remote section of India, she dedicated herself to

8

mysterious Krishna, the happy god who played the flute and encouraged young people to devote themselves to the joys of love . . ."

"Then Lola was sent home to England. But civilization could not change the wild animal grace of her bearing, the bold challenge in her flashing violet eyes, the lilt of her full sensuous mouth. About her, there lingered a subtle invitation . . . that no 'civilized' man could resist!"

I went into the bathroom and let the cold water run over my wrists for a while. Then I came back and read on:

"Many men were drawn to this strange woman, but only in one of them did Lola find an elemental force as powerful as her own. He was young, handsome Lord Jeffery Lundy. He worshipped power and evil, and he demanded of Lola the very things she was most unwilling to give. From the moment their eyes first met, a tension grew between them—a tension that finally exploded in a breath-taking crashing climax almost without equal in modern fiction!"

After wiping my chin dry I found myself prowling the room restlessly. The obvious thing to do was to get a flash-o-gram off to D. B. Carlton immediately and start Lola rolling west.

After all, Lola was a product of India, and these days we should all know more about India. Students of international affairs agree that an understanding of India, including the remote sections where mysterious Krishna hangs out, is requisite to intelligent discussion of global problems.

Besides, in a P.S. to his chatty letter, D. B. Carlton writes: "This special offer is being made to a limited number of people who enjoy good reading."

9

The man has faith in me. And now that Mr. Carlton reminds me, I do enjoy good reading and for some time have felt vaguely unsatisfied by Little Orphan Annie. I think I am ready for Lola Montero.

On the other hand I can't help wondering how D. B. Carlton got my name and knew that I was ripe for Lola, who "deliberately gave her passionate embraces to whoever needed her most." I don't remember being on any parties with a D. B. Carlton. There was a fellow named Carson in Lethbridge that I and a couple of W. D.'s . . . but then his first name was Fred.

So I've asked Mr. Shott that lives next door if he got a flash-o-gram from D. B. Carlton, and by golly he did. He remembered the picture of the infinite woman clearly. And asking around, I've discovered that D. B. Carlton of Toronto has included pretty well everybody in our block in the limited number of people who enjoy good reading, including old Mrs. Stevens who died three months ago.

That's given me pause. I think I had better read the rest of that small print. Let's see now, where was I? "From the moment their eyes first met, a tension grew between them . . ."

THE PET CORNER

ToDAY we start our Pet Corner. Animal lovers whose pets have problems are invited to write in and see if they get an answer.

Our first letter today is from a Mrs. Hugo Yourway of Ailgo Mine. Mrs. Yourway writes:

Dear Sir,

We have a canary called Mario but he will not sing. He only opens his beak to eat. He eats much more than the man said he would. We have tried playing records for Mario to see if they suggest anything. He just listens and when the records are finished he cleans his feet.

Mario cost us three dollars and my husband says if he does not sing soon he will find him a cat to play with.

Do you know how to make him sing?

(Mrs.) Hugo Yourway.

P.S. We do not know whether Mario is a boy or a girl. Should that make any difference?

Dear Mrs. Yourway,

Some canaries don't know when they are well off. I suggest you ignore Mario for a few days. Give him no food. Let his apple get wrinkly. After a while he'll make some sort of noise, even if it's just knocking his head against the bars of his cage.

Whether Mario is a boy or a girl canary should make no difference to his or her singing, but it might be just as well not to discuss the matter in the bird's presence. Some canaries don't say anything but they can hear like nobody's business.

11

. . . the best method is to have your dog's teeth removed.

TWICE OVER LIGHTLY

Second Letter:

Dear Mr. Nicholls,

Our dog bites postmen.

We have had six different postmen in the last year and our dog has bitten them all. He gets them when they bend over to put the letters in the slot.

He doesn't mean anything by it but you can see they don't like it. Is there anything you can do to stop a dog from biting postmen?

Otto Waugh.

Dear Mr. Waugh,

Stopping a dog from biting postmen is fairly simple. One way is to give the dog some letters to carry and while he is carrying them, *you* bite *him*. This will give him the postman's point of view and get your name in the papers, especially if the dog dies of hydrophobia.

Another way is to wean the dog onto policemen. But possibly the best method is to have your dog's teeth removed. Very few dogs find fulfilment in gumming a postman.

Third Letter:

Dear Sir,

Our tortoise, Jim, has just laid an egg. We have had Jim for ten years and he has never done it before. He hasn't had anything to play with except gravel. We hate to change his name now because he is just getting used to it and when called will snap at your finger.

In the meantime we have this egg in the middle of the rug. We don't know whether to move it or not because we don't know how Jim feels about it, since he has gone upstairs. What do you suggest?

Mrs. W. C. Overflow.

Dear Mrs. Overflow,

There's no point in trying to hush this thing up. I suggest you take another look at Jim's gravel. Then you should inspect the egg closely. If it has a black spot on it, it is a billiard ball and Jim is having his little joke. You need not hesitate to move a billiard ball as long as you use the end of the cue and don't put your leg on the table.

Yours,

The Pet Corner.

NOTE: Don't forget, friends, that Be Kind to Animals Week is May 6th to 12th. You still have plenty of time in which to beat the stuffing out of the little rascals.

SPRING!

THE COMING of spring is traditionally the occasion for newspaper columnists to leap about like lambs, bleating their joy in the rejuvenation of the earth.

I guess I'm about the last to leap this year. I'm not as lamby as I used to be and I have to take a run at it. But a couple of afternoons ago, as I was walking up Seymour in the bright sunshine, spring suddenly hit me. After a few preliminary gurgles the sap began to flow. Waiting for the light at Pender, I filled my lungs with air, causing the woman next to me to edge away nervously. Yes, every sense confirmed the presence of the oldest living miracle. It was spring again.

As I walked along I felt springier and springier, smiling at all the young women who were wearing their shadows shorter. Those that felt the spring smiled back, but quite a few were still in the grip of winter.

Happily I watched the signs of spring multiply— the old gents repossessing Victory Square from the seagulls, the clearance sales of wedding rings, the clarion exhortations to change my oil, the news that Tommy Manville was marrying again.

Spring brings its own special light, a warm, golden glow. In this light the girl who, during winter, loved and lost, looks lovelier than ever. And the girl who

15

won without loving seems to be wearing too much make-up.

In the light of spring the junior clerk who has just given too much to the Red Cross, and discovered the strange elation of giving too much, takes on a radiance that the ignorant blame on his necktie.

It's spring because in the residential districts the forsythia has turned yellow, and so has the margarine, and the roads are a mass of spring potholes. At the house where the children have played on the front lawn all winter, sliding in the snow and heeling the tender sod, the grass grows thick and green again, while the crusty gentleman with the fence and the dog stares grumpily at his balding sward without seeing that it is infected with malice.

It's spring because the days are getting longer, along with the faces of the skiers, and the faces of the students lost in the forest of exams.

It's spring because the sky is restless, the clouds, still wild with winter, running this way and that, beset by the sheep-dog winds.

It's spring because the first blowfly drones through the house, sounding the key for sleepy summer, sitting on the sunlit window and rubbing his palms together in anticipation of all the picnics to which he isn't invited.

Some of the sounds of spring are subtler. Such as the quick rasp of the golfer cleaning his repaints with his wife's nail brush. Or the protesting creak of the cricketer's climbing into the old white flannels for another season. Or, subtlest of all, the unspoken words of young lovers strolling arm-in-arm in the

16

night, for the language of spring is phrased by the eyes and punctuated with kisses.

Yes, sir, spring's my season. You can have autumn. I leave you the last chrysanthemum and press upon myself the first daffodil, the first flower of spring (the crocus is not so much a flower as a punk of colour to touch off the floral fireworks). Through the million megaphones of daffodils spring is shouted to the world. Spring . . . !

There, you see, the exclamation points are coming up. My prose is growing lush and I seem to hear an editor oiling his shears. I don't care. What does an editor know of spring? Does an editor know the painful ecstasy of wanting to build a nest before the trees are in leaf? Does he think I'm running around with this bit of string in my mouth just for laughs?

So, hey nonny nonny, every drake to his duck, and a goose for the gander, and who will be queen of the May?

I SIPPED WITH NELSON

THE OTHER evening I was invited to a cocktail party in honour of Mr. Nelson Eddy. When you're a newspaper columnist you get invited to things like that. It is what you have instead of money, a home, wife, kids, security and the respect of the community.

That is why newspaper columnists at these cocktail parties drink like drains, their beady eyes flickering about the room in search of food. A veteran columnist can be deeply engrossed in what a celebrity is saying and at the same time be reaching one arm around a fat lady to shag an olive. The writing part is easy.

As soon as I entered the hotel reception room where the cocktail party was being held, I recognized Nelson Eddy. He didn't recognize me, or if he did he didn't let on. Nobody else seemed to recognize me either (the room was pretty smoky), so I slipped into my aloof, spectator-of-life's-follies pose.

When I find myself alone at a party I always play this aloof role in which I like to think I resemble George Sanders. The resemblance has so far escaped other people, who instead take me for a waiter that is shirking his duty.

So I was glad when a waiter brought me a drink and a lady came up to say:

"Excuse me, but I just want to tell you how much I enjoy reading your column."

"Well, thank you," I laughed, letting the monocle fall out of my eye.

"But," she said, "you don't look at all like your pictures, Mr. Ruark."

"I look different if you take me into the daylight," I snarled.

Another waiter offered me a trayful of the little loaded crackers that they always have at cocktail parties, and I was upset enough to take one. These nerve-testers comprise a cracker the size of a fifty-cent piece, covered with a layer of paste in which are imbedded shrimps supporting a pickle on which rolls an onion in constant, uneasy motion.

The trick is to get all this into your mouth without having a shrimp or pickle do a one-and-a-half gainer into your drink and spray rye into your eye. I was just wiping my eye when my host invited me over to meet Nelson Eddy.

Mr. Eddy and I shook hands and I said:

"I hope you'll enjoy your stay in Vancouver," and the eye with the rye in it winked at him.

"I hope I can get my laundry done," Mr. Eddy said, a bit wanly.

"You shouldn't have any trouble there," I said, winking like crazy.

Mr. Eddy and I sort of drifted apart then. As he turned his back I noticed that we were both wearing suits of green shark's tooth, only my shark's tooth came from farther back in the mouth.

I was also struck by his extreme youthfulness. He looked as though he might at any moment strip off his green suit to reveal buckskin, snatch Jeanette Macdonald from under a table and ride off yodelling excerpts from "Naughty Marietta."

"Did you meet him?" a young lady asked me, in passing.

"Yes," I said, "He's still young-looking, isn't he? Looks just the same as he did in 'Rose Marie.' "

"I guess so," she said. "That was before my time."

I got another drink. Then the photographers arrived and posed a picture of Mr. Eddy offering a trayful of loaded crackers to a little girl.

"Lickety, pickety, schmickety, nickety, poo," Mr. Eddy said, the little girl smiled, and the picture was taken. Mr. Eddy then went back to talking to a somewhat older little girl, one in a low-cut gown.

About that time I found myself slipping into George Sanders again, so I treated the room to one last mocking glance and made for the elevator.

I shall, naturally, report to you on any other celebrities I hobnob with, and you must tell me about interesting people *you* meet. Deal?

GHOST CARS ARE UN-CANADIAN

Drivers can no longer depend on "spotting" a police car and driving accordingly.

Out on our streets now are some prowl cards which look just like tens of thousands of other cars. They're various colours and the sirens and other familiar police gadgets can't be seen.

Chief Constable Mulligan said when the department has a full complement of cars, 25 will be of various colours.

—NEWS ITEM.

THIS time they have gone too far.

It was bad enough when they took off their tunics so that we couldn't see the buttons shining from a distance.

It was bad enough when they gave up the pursuit of thieves and murderers to devote themselves more fully to chalking noughts and crosses on the tires of parked cars.

Now they are going to camouflage their prowl cars to look like guilty motorists, so that we can't tell friend from foe, so that they can sneak up on us. Talk about shooting ducks in a barrel! The police force has lost its sporting spirit and found that of a weasel.

Many a time I have been cruising at a crisp 30 past a school—one of those modern schools fiendishly designed to look like a California ranch, or a Swedish gas station, or anything but a school—when I have noticed in my mirror a siren surfacing in the traffic, or the bloodshot eye of a prowl blinker peering at me.

In an instant I have slowed to 10 miles an hour, if not actually stopped to lead the children by the hand across the street, distributing jelly beans and wearing the benign look of the man who adores kiddies. Those old black police cars brought out the best in me.

Now the first I'll know of approaching pirates will be when some cop fires a maroon sedan across my bow, before I can even bring up my jelly beans.

Well, they'll be sorry.

The next step after painting the cars different colours and hiding the gadgets, will be the shucking of even the vestiges of uniform. If the ladies will kindly remove their hats I shall now run a lantern slide of an episode in the future of Vancouver's chameleon constabulary.

A fuchsia convertible with lime sidewall tires and a jungle of mohair monkeys dancing in the rear window rockets past a blue Volkswagon and nips it screaming to the curb. Two men slide out of the convertible, one zoot-suited in sea-green, the other mostly concealed by a sombrero and the large sunflower in his buttonhole.

Producing the pencil on the end of the long chain looping to his ankle, one man puts the bright yellow point of his shoe on the Volkswagon's runningboard.

Cop 1: All right, where do you think you're going—to a fire?

Driver (*steaming his own hat, a Tyrolean trilby, with rage*): Yes, dammit, I am.

Cop 2 (*at the other door, speaking thickly through his petals*): Oh, a wise guy, eh?

DRIVER (*jumping up and down with rage*): You lummoxes! Don't you recognize a police sergeant when you see one?

(*The two cops lean into the car, gaze at the driver's feet quivering hugely on the floor, and retract ashen faces*).

COP 2: Gosh, Sarge, we didn't know—

DRIVER: Know, schmoe! You're through. Go back to the station and turn in your sunflower.

(*Cop 1, his lips budded to kiss the sergeant's paw, almost loses his nose as the Volkswagon reverses and roars away. The two cops slouch back to the convertible, whose windshield bears a ticket for parking near a hydrant. Swaying away from the car is what looks like a lady of the evening, except for her charm bracelet of handcuffs. The two cops quietly take their summons books and beat one another over the head with them*).

CURTAIN

Moral: No good can come from the police's being as crafty as the motorists. Britain has the best motorists in the world, and the English bobby wearing his inverted bucket and pumping his bicycle can be identified as soon as the curvature of the earth permits him to come into view.

It isn't British, Chief Mulligan.

A SURFEIT OF TALENT

THAT fountain of fact, *Life* magazine, devotes part of a recent issue to a feature entitled "The Quandary of a Gifted Girl." This girl, 18-year-old Phyllis Newell of Forest Hills, Long Island, is an expert pianist, does creditable ceramics, makes $15 an hour as a model, has a boy friend, and can't make up her mind which aptitude to develop. She just has too many talents, the poor kid.

Miss Newell's predicament reminds me of a similar case, the quandary of a gifted boy—me.

Miss Newell, *Life* says, was playing the piano at 4 and composing tunes at 5. I, too, was playing at 4. (My parents say I was 13, but they are insanely jealous.) I wasn't playing the piano, of course. I played the drums. Actually these drums were pots of various sizes which I hauled out of the pantry and beat with pieces of kindling.

Needless to say the family recognized that I had something and they looked for some place to send me. The only school that taught how to play the drums required that the pupils supply their own drums, so the family bought me a set of traps and waited for me to go away. The drums were too heavy for my tiny arms to carry, however, so that it was simpler for the family to run away from home.

But already my multitude of talents were savagely

24

It was simpler for the family to run away from home.

fighting each other for supremacy. Miss Newell, *Life* says, was doing promising drawings and paintings when she was 6. This is a remarkable coincidence, since I too was doing drawings and paintings when she was 6. (I was 20.) I had then been in the high school art class for several years, working on the project of drawing a straight line through two points without missing one of them.

Some of my drawings reminded the teacher of Jean Miro, the abstractionist, but more of them reminded her of Mr. Bagfoss, the principal, and I was thrown out of the class.

This break with academic art failed to ruffle me, since like Miss Newell, I found painting "not enough of a challenge." After all, it had been done. Rubens had done it, Utrillo had done it, Uncle Fred had done it. (Uncle Fred painted nudes. He put the gold paint on the exotic dancers at Minsky's and was insisting on applying a second coat one night when he was killed.)

Of Miss Newell, *Life* continues: "At 13 her beauty had blossomed, she became a model for junior fashions." Miss Newell nosed me out there. I was 16 before my beauty blossomed (it was the spring of '16 and I was a riot of colour).

Thus was the dilemma of which of my many gifts to exploit complicated by the heavy demand for me as a professional model. The manufacturers of tonics and kidney pills trampled each other to get my photo to illustrate that dull, logy, pepless feeling. My potentials as a model were described as limitless, especially after I broke out in pimples and went bald on one side of my head.

"Recently a new factor entered to complicate her future further: Phyllis now has a steady beau." I know how Phyllis feels. I was still torn between drumming, painting and modelling when a new factor named Elsinore McGirth entered to complicate my future. Elsinore was old enough to be my mother, but there was something about her that fascinated me every time she opened her wallet. Though I limited myself to seven dates a week with her, I began to think seriously about marriage.

Then war! When I listed my many talents to the R.C.A.F. enlistment officer he nodded and put me down for general duties. I arrived at the Toronto Manning Depot to take up my duties as a general, maps under my arm and lumps of sugar in my pocket for my horse, but they handed me a broom and told me to sweep out the sheep pen.

Since the war I have been writing to fill in while waiting for the old talents to reassert themselves. They aren't rushing into it. In fact I would go so far as to recommend to Miss Newell that she marry that steady beau. It's a lot better to throw up a career than to have *it* throw *you* up. Look out below!

NO, I DON'T WANT TO HOLD HIM

An awful lot of my friends seem to be having babies. I suppose if they had to have something, babies are the least of several evils. But sometimes I wish I could see the other evils before finally making up my mind.

Like most other bachelors, I find babies completely terrifying. I will walk a mile to avoid a baby, probably to find another baby waiting for me when I get there. In the movies, when the screen is offering a close-up of a baby and everybody around me is oohing and ahing, I am quietly hissing and showing my teeth. I also am not amused by talcum ads.

The main reason babies make me uncomfortable is that I don't know how they work. They are so very helpless, yet not quite helpless enough to suit me. They have a sort of persistent, flailing strength that enables them sooner or later to get hold of your tie and choke you.

The trouble is, as soon as people have a baby they develop a blind spot. They forget people have been having babies more or less like theirs since Eve took to apples, and will go on having them for a while yet. They think that what they've got in the basket is unique, that you'll want to see it and die.

New parents are of two kinds. There's the proud-and-we-don't-care-who-knows-it type. And there's the

we-don't-make-a-fuss-over-it type. The second type
is, if anything, more dangerous than the first, since
the parents consider it the height of indifference to
pay no attention when the baby hurls a building
block into your eye. As far as they are concerned the
baby can go on bonking you with blocks all night—
the little rascal won't get any praise from *them*.

My own policy regarding babies is never to enter
a house in which there is anyone under 21 years of
age. I don't mind meeting babies in the street, where
I can get a good run-back or can work around so that
the sun is in their eyes.

Even so, I blunder into homes where babies lurk.
Just the other evening I found myself trapped in an
apartment with an infant a month old and a mother
and father under the delusion that their baby
exhibited some special features and conveniences not
found on other models.

They also seemed to mistake me for the sort of
potential father who would be fascinated by these
latest developments, and I was repeatedly called from
one room into the other to inspect "his cute iddle
nose," then "his cute iddle tummy," then "his cute
iddle toes" and various other flotsam and jetsam
including a rumble seat.

At least if it wasn't his seat that was rumbling,
something certainly was. His mother said he had the
burps. Disgusting. The child obviously had only
one way of expressing itself, or two at the most, and
neither of them struck me as being anything to be
proud of.

Babies don't reach their full strength of obnox-
iousness, however, until the age of about 18 months.

By that time they are able to crawl or stagger, always towards me. The reverse of radishes, I don't like babies but they like me. Embarrassment heightens the redness of my nose and babies can't resist it. They tear their play-pens apart to get at me.

Fixed of eye and slobbering, they come at me with the stiff gait of a robot.

"He likes you!" carol the parents, as though this were to my greater glory. "Go see Uncle Eric," they say. "Go see Uncle Eric."

And Uncle Eric grins and says: "Well, he's certainly grown, hasn't he?"

One thing about being approached by a Bengal tiger is you don't have to sit there grinning and saying: "Well, he's certainly grown, hasn't he?"

When the baby finally reaches me, as it always does, I try to thwart its attempts to get its cute iddle pinkies into my dirty old mouth. I dandle it on my knee. Babies love being dandled, and Uncle Eric dandles baby on his knee so long that by the time he gets home the joint's jumpin'.

Well, bad habits being as tenacious as they are, I guess people will go on having babies. But this is fair warning that one of these days I am going to bite one of the iddle darlings right in his iddle leg.

THE SWAMP

I WAS sorry to read that a group of parents had a meeting to demand removal of the old Swamp.

When I was Huck Finn's age, the Swamp was my Mississippi. Our house was just a quiet block from the woods in which it lay, like another world, a world filled with menace and magic. The world of adults and arithmetic ended at Sixteenth and Camosun. After that it was every cowboy for himself.

The woods in which the Swamp lived were about a hundred yards thick, a fierce tangle of maple and cedar and the rearing monsters of stump roots. Here a cowboy could hunt an Indian with only such dangers to himself as he bade his imagination create.

But beyond! Beyond the woods lay the Swamp. As a cowboy crept down the trail to that awful bog, his imagination took over. As the maples and cedars gave way to the heavy, snatching undergrowth, and the solid trail narrowed suddenly to the spongy floor of the Swamp, a cowboy reined up. A cowboy thought he heard Things coming from the opposite direction, slithering, gaping Things that lived on small cowboys. And a cowboy would turn and, abandoning his horse for greater speed, run like a rabbit for home.

For a time I risked only the fringe of the Swamp, where the skinny brown arms of water curled around reeds and rotting logs. I and a couple of other squibs practised a drainage programme of a sort, taking

Here a cowboy could hunt an Indian.

home a jam jar of swamp water evening after evening, the amber water alive with darting polliwogs.

The jam jars were emptied into a roomy oil barrel in the backyard. There the polliwogs swarmed in ever greater numbers, grew legs, dropped tails, hopped out in their hundreds and chirped off back to the Swamp to provide us with the next year's hunting.

But the middle of the Swamp remained the unknown, the sinister. Not until I was about nine did I follow some adventurous companions along one of the spongy, twisting paths that led to the heart of the Swamp. I was scared. The runt pines were just big enough to conceal a scaly beast. The path was potholed with black, sucking pits of water that my companions announced to be bottomless. I felt the perspiring terror of the cowboy who realizes that the six-shooter on his hip will just sink him that much faster to China.

Then, there it was, the round brown eye of the Swamp, the dead and deadly centre. A few water lilies dappling the scum. A half-sunken raft. A rim of ooze that my friends informed me was quicksand. I have never been so light on my feet, before or since, as I was that day in the Swamp, suspended, like a dragonfly, inches above the ground, by sheer beating of the wings of fear.

After that I entered the Swamp more often, nibbling its blueberries in summer, sliding along its icy lanes in winter. But for me the Swamp never lost its aura of the unearthly. When, as an older boy, I accidentally plunged a leg down one of the potholes, my first thought was that I had hit the bottomless.

I don't know exactly what part of my being was conditioned by the experience of the Swamp. But I know it's in there somewhere. Probably every kid has this experience of the frightening encounter with the demon, the little private struggle that must be won. He should. The demon is much harder to lick when he gets older.

Now that I am old enough to know that the Swamp was always innocent, that it was just a little whim of nature, it is curious to hear a group of adults denounce it as a killer. But, I suppose if it poisoned those kiddies with polio, or even if it is suspect, it will have to go.

In its defence I will say only that it is not the Swamp but the sewage men have fouled it with that is criminal. Nature never intended the Swamp for men's sewage. She intended it for polliwogs and small cowboys like me. It was a wonderful place to grow up.

A MAN AND HIS STRAWBERRY

I BELIEVE in giving credit where credit is due, so here's a hymn to the strawberry.

The strawberry season began about five weeks ago. I believe I have eaten one or two other things since, but mostly I've been eating strawberries. When I stick out my tongue it looks like a strawberry and I've bitten it a couple of times by mistake. I'm crazy for strawberries.

The first strawberries, a month ago, were from California. They looked like strawberries but they didn't have much flavour. That was because they were forced. You can't force a strawberry. It is a voluptuous fruit and loves to be coaxed.

The strawberries we are getting now, I am told, come from Victoria. You can follow the birds to Victoria and tail the strawberries back. Bravo, Victoria! Your strawberries are so large, luscious and flavourful that we readily forgive you for the layers of wormy little green ones on which the big red one sits.

Soon we shall have mainland strawberries, and then—O, rapture, thy name is *Fragaria vesca*—strawberries from our own back yard. The strawberry patch is ready for them. The clean yellow straw lies thick about the plants to foil the worm. The netting hangs above them to fox the robin. Skilled hands have tenderly worked the soil about them. Not *my* skilled hands, of course. My part in the preparation is to sit with my great red mouth agape, waiting. I am salivating beautifully.

One day soon they will be ready for the picking. Picking strawberries has much of the excitement of finding somebody else's golf ball.

The plant tries to hide her fruit. She offers a small strawberry here, a small strawberry there, and suddenly, moving aside a bit of straw, we find her treasure, her masterpiece, snuggled against the earth, ripely red (another day would have been too late), heavy in the hand, bulging at its succulent seams, as rich a prize as any plump houri stolen from the sheik's tent.

It should go into the bowl with the others. Of course it should. It's the only decent thing to do. A strawberry like that should be shared with the rest of the family. Really.

(Hahahahahahaha. Mm, that was good! Wonder if there's another one?)

Picking strawberries is also a fine way to carry on a delicate conversation. You can say some pretty searching things if you're peering into a strawberry plant.

I remember picking strawberries behind a cottage in Kent, while discussing with a sprightly lady the love life of her niece, in whom I was interested at the time. I finished with a pan full of berries and the knowledge that the niece had done her picking and I was still on the bush.

Once the strawberries have been picked they must be taken into the house and the stems removed. I have found that the best way to remove the stems from strawberries is to wash each strawberry individually, then dip the damp berry into a bowl of sugar and pop it into the mouth, holding onto the stem until each berry has disappeared. This way you don't have to touch the strawberry with the hands. Very sanitary.

Strawberries must never be served with milk. This is a luxurious fruit that must have fitting company. Devonshire cream and sour cream are worthy of admission to the presence, but a strawberry is exalted to its greatest glory only by the whipping cream of a strawberry short cake, that sublime temple of taste before which even the most dedicated dieter must finally bow in reverence.

I don't get tired of strawberries. Once, when I was a kid, I had the hives and somebody blamed them on too many strawberries. I remember that I felt miserable, not because I would have to give up strawberries but because I would have to go through life with the hives. I thought I would lose a lot of time scratching that could have been spent eating strawberries.

The hives gave up. And now, as my tongue badgers the familiar seed in my teeth, I agree with Izaak Walton's Dr. Boteler, who said of strawberries, "Doubtless God could have made a better berry, but doubtless God never did."

TYPES OF PEDESTRIANS:
A RUN-DOWN

A FEW MONTHS ago, as a pedestrian, I considered motorists to be the most dangerous gang of ruffians ever let loose on humanity.

Since then I have bought a car and I now see that pedestrians, not motorists, are the world's most exasperating bunch of knuckleheads.

A large part of this nastiness of pedestrians seems to stem from the law's revision to give the pedestrian the right of way so completely that the motorist feels compelled to slow down before he even climbs into bed with his wife.

Pedestrians comprise a variety of queer birds. The following is a partial Audubon of species of pedestrians, based on close and apoplectic observation.

The Trolleycatcher—usually appears in numbers around dusk, while motorist is in a line of cars waiting for light to change. Darts from curb, between cars, sometimes running along bumper in frantic effort to catch bus or street car. Average life span: short.

The Crosswalker (or North American ostrich)—Frequents space between two yellow lines painted on road. Ignores traffic, aware of being in a sanctuary.

When car is approaching, often deliberately looks in opposite direction, slows pace, reads newspaper, or sets up light housekeeping in middle of road. Dies with smile on face, knowing it has been hit out of bounds.

The Jaybird—Very common in Chinatown but liable to pop out anywhere. A cunning bird, owing to the $5 fine for jay-walking. Often visible only as a head peering around parked car to see if motorist is a police ghost car. If motorist is not police car, will run to middle of street and get itself trapped between two streams of traffic, from which position it is liable to run anywhere.

The Pileated Lightbeater—Prides itself on ability to judge when red light will turn green. If light is late turning green, steps out regardless. Spirit of independence often mentioned in obituary.

The Ruffled Grouse—Usually an old specimen, male. Goes for long walks through heavy traffic to indulge hatred for automobiles. Takes any sound of auto horn as personal attack. Favourite habitat: with a flock of fellow pedestrians thwarting motorist's attempt to get around a corner before the signal changes. Cry: a loud squawk, usually to the editor of a newspaper.

(This species not to be confused with the *Tweedy Cane-packer,* a British variety that slashes at American-make cars because of something Senator McCarthy has said.)

The Hitch-hiker—A bold bird that travels on its thumb. If picked up by motorist, will ask why motorist hasn't traded car in for later model. Usually male, but pairs of females sometimes seen, identifiable by glasses and giggles.

The Horned Gasser—Always found in pairs, pair having recognized each other in middle of intersection and stopped for chat. Ignores auto horn. Often is still talking after being run over.

The Nighthatch—Noctural, favouring highways and walking on the right (i.e. wrong) side of road, with no tail-light. Livens up traffic by forcing cars into middle of road.

The Gamp-crested Blunderbusser—Observed only in wet weather. Usually female, large, with bundles. Crosses street with head inside umbrella, watching own feet. Major improvement over old-fashioned sitting duck, but liable to leave windshield covered with vegetables.

Adam's Pigeon—Named after discoverer. Female. Usually observed waiting for bus. Pretty legs. Delicate colouring. Inviting smile. Of no help as motorist tries to replace lamp-post he has rammed.

Well, I hope that students of outdoor life will find this catalogue useful. Since I have figured out how much my car is costing me to run, they may expect a similar treatise on motorists as observed by a pedestrian (male Great-Beaked Bushwhacker).

THE GAMP-CRESTED
BLUNDER BUSTER

THE TWEEDY CANE-PACKER

THE HORNED GASSER

THE RUFFLED GROUSE

THE TROLLEYCATCHER

THE PILEATED LIGHTBEATER

A partial Audubon of pedestrians.

BRING BACK THE SILKWORM

IN SEATTLE the other day I bought a nylon shirt and some nylon underwear. I know that I should have bought them in Canada. I hated myself in the morning. But when I see a chance to save a dollar and a half something snaps in my head and I can't remember a word of "O Canada."

Besides, there's something dashing about bringing American luxuries back across the border. Sort of riskay, especially if the stuff's hidden under the toolsay.

I don't really know why I bought nylon. Cotton has always been good enough for me. I guess I was just a mad, impetuous fool. I wanted to live as the stars live, and as everybody knows the stars live in nylon houses, swim in nylon swimming pools, and have nylon babies because they're easier to wash.

In the clear, cold light of dawn my purchases looked less sidereal. The nylon shirt proved to be mostly cardboard and stuffing. It felt like a lot of shirt in the cellophane package, but when I ripped off the cellophane and the label, took out the cardboard and tissue paper, removed the celluloid band inside the collar, and disarmed the shirt of its pins, most of my $8.95 seemed to be lying in the wastebasket.

When I tried the shirt on I was alarmed to see

in the mirror that it was transparent. The transparent blouse can look quite fetching on the opposite sex (women), but on me it could merely reveal that I didn't have a clean undershirt to put on. I have never considered it to be any advantage to a man to look diaphanous. Women see through me quickly enough as it is. I don't need a filmy chemise to expose my nasty plans.

As for the nylon underwear, it makes a funny noise when I walk. It squeaks. I suppose it's the metallic thread chafing my trousers, but I don't like it. I love attracting attention as much as the next man, but not by making a noise like a fat girl crossing her legs 120 to the minute. There's always some catch to these miracles of science. You don't have to iron this underwear but it squeaks when you walk. All I need to go with it is a pair of squawky shoes and I'd sound like the Hoosier Hotshots.

The nylon underwear also builds up a lot of static electricity. My old underwear just fell away and could be drop-kicked briskly onto a chair. The nylon must be fought off, like peeling a whale, and I've had to put my foot on it to get it off my hand. Some people may think it's fun to finish undressing in a shower of sparks, but with me it has just deepened my affection for the silkworm.

The result of all this has been to disenchant me as far as nylon is concerned. I used to think of it as a magic tissue possessing the power to open doors. That was in London where the women were desperate for good nylon stockings. A man with his own apartment and an independent supply of nylons from

Canada could cut quite a swath in London, I thought. Usually the pitch was:

"If I may say so, Miss Featherstonehaugh, you have singularly pretty stems. What a pity to waste them in grass hockey stockings! Allow me to present you with a pair of sheerest nylons from the bazaars of fabled Granville Street."

Miss Featherstonehaugh's gracious acceptance ("Orl right") meant an order for one pair of nylons to be shipped from home base. Unfortunately the stockings took three weeks to arrive, in which time Miss Featherstonehaugh had usually discovered the American downstairs who owned a Renaud runabout. I massed a fair stock of nylons in odd sizes. Only once or twice was I able to complete the benefaction and savour the role of *homme du monde*.

That was how I developed my profound respect for the power of nylon, a veneration only slightly shaken when my dentist told me to avoid toothbrushes with nylon bristles because they spiked the gums. What we lost on the gums we gained on the gams. I remained a disciple.

But now that I've tried wearing nylon I feel that it is strictly for the ladies. Clinching this belief, somebody has told me that nylon disintegrates in the presence of sulphur in the air. Much as I hope to go to Heaven, I'm afraid I'd better buy an all-purpose wardrobe.

THE WELL-REJECTED WRITER

SOMETIMES I go to the mirror on the wall and say:

"Mirror, mirror on the wall,
Who is the funniest writer of them all?"

And the mirror replies: "Fred Allen."

That is what I get for buying a cheap mirror and putting it in the same room with the radio.

I put up with the smart-aleck mirror because I know it doesn't know any better, but I am still shaken by rejection slips.

This week I got a manuscript back with a rejection slip. It shook me.

You go along selling a piece here, a piece there, and pretty soon you get to think you're a writer. You wear your hat on the back of your head and you're fairly offhand when the high school annual asks you for a contribution. Maybe you grow a beard like Ernest Hemingway, or develop a limp like Somerset Maugham. In my case I developed pimples like Noel Cowpath, the wit of Matsqui.

Then one day you get a rejection slip and your beard falls off, or your pimples dry up. You are ravaged by self-doubt. You look in the mirror and ask yourself if you're finished. Too old to start afresh, you think. Nothing to look forward to but the old-age pension and what you can get for your stamp collection.

In your mind you phrase the letter they will find in the sad, gas-filled room. Nothing self-pitying, mind you. Nothing flowery. Just 450 pages of beautiful writing, showing the diamond-hard incisiveness of genius and a philosophical insight that will make Wilde's *De Profundis* look like *Tiger Tim*.

After a while, of course, you get over it. Reason displaces dank despair. You realize that editors can make mistakes. You can't expect an editor to appreciate a writer who is ahead of his time. Look at James Joyce and Gertrude Stein. It was years before editors recognized their talent. Look at Noel Cowpath. Editors *still* don't recognize his talent, just because he writes single-space on a shingle with a nail.

As for me, I've had rejection slips before. Every successful writer says that at the beginning he got so many rejection slips he could paper his room with them. So, when I began writing I also started papering my room with the rejection slips I received. I'd got only one wall finished, however, when I sold something. Naturally I was furious. My room, which had four walls at the time, was left looking messy. I felt I had slipped up somewhere.

I was glad to get that first cheque, though. I framed it and began writing with redoubled vigour. This was rewarded by redoubled rejection slips. After a month I took the cheque out of the frame and cashed it. After another month I sold the frame. I moved into a smaller room whose walls would be easier to paper and began all over.

I also remember my first job of radio writing.

The CBC hired me to write *Stag Party* after Alan Young left. Young had built the show up so that it was carried by the Trans-Canada network and NBC blue network. I started writing it, and in two shows we lost the NBC blue network. In three more shows we lost the CBC eastern network. A half-dozen shows after that we were down to members of our immediate families, and even they were fidgety.

In the thirteen shows of the series I wrote, *Stag Party* executed the most exciting strip tease, dropping listeners right down to the bare transmitter, in the history of broadcasting.

But I was young and hard to discourage. I read an ad in a magazine headed WHO SAYS YOU CAN'T WRITE? I wrote like a madman for a year and was then able to send the magazine a list of fifty names of people who said I couldn't write. The magazine rejected it.

Now that I'm older, these rejection slips hit me harder. I've lost that old bounce, whereas my manuscripts haven't. After all, when a writer reaches a certain age it is ludicrous for him to get rejection slips. He's supposed to get testimonial dinners, the part later being played by Robert Donat.

I must remember to bring this up at the next union meeting, if we have one.

THE DRIVE-IN MENACE

As though there weren't enough happening around to keep me jumpy, the paper says we can expect more drive-in banks in Canada.

I suppose that sooner or later they will open a drive-in bank in our district. They needn't hurry on my account. If there's one thing I don't need it's a drive-in bank. I hardly need an ordinary bank. I can always go to the post office to fill my pen.

Frankly, I don't see how a drive-in bank could work. Of course, I didn't see how a drive-in restaurant and drive-in theatre would work either. If I had been around in the 19th century when Paul Muni was inventing pasteurized milk, I would have scoffed at him, too. I never learn.

The truth is the drive-in restaurant and drive-in theatre *don't* work as far as I am concerned. When somebody slides a tray of food across the front seat of my car at nose level, I get the feeling I am eating under the table, and I usually get the business of turning my lights on and off all balled up. As for the drive-in theatre, I haven't been back since I arrived home from one and found its loud-speaker still hanging inside my window. To me, no drive-in movie is worth having to sneak into the back yard in the middle of the night to bury a loud-speaker.

A drive-in bank would be even more impractical

48

for me, since I have never really mastered either driving or banking. Each is a full-time job for me while I'm at it.

People who try to talk to me while I'm driving, for instance, often have to wait several minutes for an answer if I happen to be waiting for a light to change. Several romances have been nipped in the bud when the young woman beside me has said something tender and I have just sat staring at the ammeter on the dashboard, wondering why the needle was bobbing around like that.

People who speak to me in the bank are even less likely to get an answer. I enter the bank with complete confidence that it is about to become the scene for an amusing farce in which I shall play the lead. Sometimes my role is simply that of trying to accept a pen from the teller and getting my hand jammed under the wicket. Or, in a more elaborate production, I may go to the teller I have always gone to, disregarding the fact that she is now the manager's secretary and he doesn't want me hanging around his office. Often I've wished a couple of thugs would come in and hold up the bank, just to create a diversion.

That's how I know that a drive-in bank would flummox me completely. I'd hand the car-hop my money and drive straight into the vault. There'd be broken computers for blocks. No drive-in bank could afford to have me as a customer. They'd cut off my blotters in no time.

To be blunt, I don't see why we need drive-in banks in the first place. Drive-in motels, drive-in restaurants, drive-in movies, drive-in banks—where will it all end? Pretty soon people won't do anything unless they can drive in, and their legs will shrivel up. I've been driving for only six months, yet only the other day a tailor told me that my legs were shorter than they should be.

As far as I can see (to the end of my nose, on a clear day), the drive-in bank will mostly be a convenience for bank robbers, who won't have to go through that business of backing out to a waiting car, which was tedious at best.

Well, I can only hope that the change-over will not be complete and that there will still be some foot banks for people like me. Otherwise it means keeping my money in my shoe, and the dimes will fall out the hole. Progress, tch.

HOMER TURNS A NEW LEAF

HOMER QUINCY had tried everything. Flowers, flattery, a flashy red convertible—everything. He still couldn't click with women.

There was something about him, something that put them off. Because there was never anything about any woman that put Homer off, he worried about this. More than anything else in the world, Homer wanted success with the ladies.

One evening, glumly reading a magazine in his room, he noticed an ad. In bright green lettering it said: "CHLOROMINTS—the only candy that kills your breath." There was a picture of a handsome young man exhaling confidently. "Chloromints contain chlorophyll," the ad went on, "the magic green substance in all growing plants that transforms the sun's energy into life-giving nourishment. Destroys MOUTH ODOUR."

Homer decided to try the sun's energy. The next day he asked the new girl in the labelling department for a date. To play safe, he asked her over the phone. She accepted, and joyfully Homer went out and bought a package of Chloromints.

The next night, before calling for the girl in the labelling department, Homer opened the vivid green package and popped one of the green tablets into his mouth. It tasted fresh and minty. Then, because it might be a long time before there was another new girl in the labelling department, Homer poured half the package into his mouth and crunched the tablets thoroughly before swallowing them. And lest the sun's energy should dissipate itself on the desert of his room, he hurried to pick up his date.

The evening was a triumph. When Homer kissed the girl goodnight she hung upon his mouth giggling. He told her that she was different from any girl he had ever known, which in view of her steel teeth was no exaggeration. After another kiss he drove home exultant.

For his next date Homer consumed a whole package of the green Chloromints and, a mass of solar energy, repeated and enlarged his previous success.

In fact it wasn't until a week after he started eating the Chloromints that he had the first hint that something was wrong. It happened when he was parked down by the beach. He leaned over to blow out the girl's match, but when his breath struck the match it flared up so dangerously she dropped it, and it would have burned her skirt but for Homer's hand.

By the time he got back to his room Homer had forgotten about the match's flaring up. Nor during the days that followed did he see anything curious in the withering of the fern plant in his room. The whiskers fell off his cactus, but he failed to associate this with his insatiable appetite for Chloromints. His girl now merely had to step into his car to start giggling and becoming light headed. Homer never even had to give her a drink.

But he did notice that he had developed the habit of chain-smoking. And, peculiarly, he never had to exhale the smoke. He drew it hungrily into his lungs and it never reappeared. To sleep comfortably he had to keep a smudge pot smoking in his room all night, with the windows closed. His craving for a smoke-filled room sharpened so severely that he thought of giving up his job at the factory and going into politics.

He gave up eating Chloromints the morning he woke up and found the little bud-like bumps on his fingers. His skin had become coarse and hard, a wrinkled brown colour, and he had become terribly stiff in the joints. It was no longer necessary to shave, but he shuffled rigidly into the bathroom, sucking a cigarette, to stare at the lobes of his ears. He saw that they were a shade greener than the day before.

Desperately seeking to ease the stiffness in his limbs, Homer drove his car to the park, parked it under the trees, clambered out and stalked slowly, stiffly towards the sunlit grass. The sun would make him feel better, he thought.

But when he came into the warm sunlight he froze in his tracks. His feet refused to move. It was as though he had been trapped by the sun. As he stood there helpless the tendrils of roots stole through the holes in his soles and grasped the earth. Almost visibly, Homer began to burgeon.

Frantic, Homer lifted his stiff arms, pleading, to heaven. They stayed there, frozen in the sun. With the horrified eyes that were already rimming into knotholes, Homer watched a young couple, strolling lost in each other's eyes, stop and sit down in his shade. And the last thing Homer saw was the girl smoothing the blanket, while the boy popped a bright green tablet into his mouth.

. . . the boy popped a bright green tablet into his mouth.

WHAT FUN TO FALL IN!

ONE highlight of the war that Eisenhower and Montgomery forgot to mention in their memoirs was compulsory drill.

Every spring, at our unit, somebody would see an airman moving slowly through an attention area on all fours, thoughtfully lipping the unlit butt of a cigarette. Whereupon the general order went out for a period of compulsory drill to smarten up our personnel.

All personnel took to the idea as a duck takes to buckshot. It was surprising, yet true, that even after six years of war, compulsory drill had not captured the imagination as a substitute for liquor or women.

When our bunch assembled on the parade square for compulsory drill they demonstrated that the gentleman who wrote the drill manual was something of a visionary, the Woodrow Wilson of the Standard Pause.

There occurred, for instance, the delightful one-act farce known as "Calling Out the Marker." Contrary to the expectations of the author of the drill manual, there was rarely any clamour of volunteering to be marker, with airmen whistling shrilly at the sergeant major and pointing to themselves, or any exhibitionism of the sort. On the contrary, when it became apparent that the sergeant major was about to call out a marker, a mass self-effacement took place on the edge of the parade square, in which everybody tried to look like a blade of grass. Everybody wanted to stand behind everybody else. A minute's work with pencil and paper proves that this movement is an impossibility, but it remained popular with servicemen.

A second purely fictional chapter in the drill manual was its account, "Fall in on the Marker." This never happened in real life. Because of the unpopularity of the positions in the front rank, a flight would as soon fall in on a leper. Actually the popular place for falling in was wherever anybody thought the middle of the centre rank would be.

Some of the dirtiest fighting of the war took place in that area, and it was always a stirring sight to watch a couple of P.F. veterans contesting the position—the clever footwork, the elbows flashing in and out, the crunch of leather on bunion and the muttered curse of the vanquished. The rear rank would become swollen with the overflow from the centre, while the front rank was mustered with difficulty, composed of the lame and the halt, the mentally infirm and a smattering of individuals who believed in promotion.

After we had fallen in we came to one of the most grisly chapters in the book, the one where the flight commander sized the flight. In cold blood. The order for that terrible havoc was, I believe, "Tallest on the right, shortest on the left, in three ranks size!" My own reaction to this order was to sit right down on the parade square and bawl. I never knew whether I was tall or short and nobody ever told me.

Then, after the front rank had numbered, I could never recall whether my file was even or odd. On one occasion I whispered to the man next to me:

"Am I odd?"

" 'Queer' is the word I would choose," he replied drily, and I sensed that he was trying to evade the question.

But by far the worst part of compulsory drill was "Mutual Instruction." This was when the sergeant handed the squad over to you. It didn't matter that you didn't want it, couldn't use it, or already had one.

Standard procedure when handed a squad to drill was (1) smirk dismally at the squad in a futile attempt to win its sympathy; (2) clear the throat noisily; (3) screech the order to quick march from a position of standing easy, quickly establishing yourself as expendable cannon fodder.

This sort of thing was supposed to give us confidence in handling men. In my own case I learned to cower at the sight of men, especially those I had obliged to march through a large puddle eight times in line, five times in threes, and once in the unusual formation that results from giving the order, "At the halt, on the left, incline your wheel, fellas!"

The drill manual was interesting reading, I suppose, but give me good old *Tom Swift and His Giant Magnet* every time.

THE WAIL BOX

(TODAY this column is taken over by Beatrice Fairfix, famous dispenser of advice to the lovelorn. Readers crushed by life's cruel wheel send in the bits to Miss Fairfix and she paints funny faces on them.) Girls should know about boys. Here is a letter from a Mr. Harold V:

Dear Miss Fairfix,

Our daughter, Gladys, is just beginning to notice boys. Since Gladys is 34 years old now we would feel better if she noticed men, like.

Gladys has always been terribly shy and blushes if you so much as mention the Isle of Man. If a person of the opposite sex comes into the house she throws her skirt over her head and runs behind the sofa where we have a terrible time getting her out.

The reason why Gladys is like this is because she had an unhappy experience when she was in her teens. One day she was climbing into a bus and an older man hit her in the shin with a grass hockey stick. Since then Gladys' knee goes out but the rest of her stays in.

The wife and I are afraid that when Gladys goes she will go sudden. I feel that her mother's efforts to tell her about men by nudges and lewd winks have only made her more confused. What should we do to get our daughter used to men? I am anxious to see Gladys happily married. Her room would make a good place for a ping-pong table.

Dear Harold V.,

You should waste no time in having Gladys learn the recognition features of the male. But you must be careful.

Chances are that Gladys is an extremely sensitive person, a tender blossom, delicately maladjusted to the world about her.

On the other hand she may be a dope.

Anyway, you might start by pointing out that *you* are a man. Possibly the girl's mother will be willing to corroborate this, or you can easily prove it by means of charts and coloured slides. Once she has accepted the idea of your being a man, you can invite some nice fellow to the house and lock Gladys in a closet with him for a couple of hours.

As for her morbid association of males with the grass hockey stick, this can be easily overcome by showing her that the grass hockey stick is, after all, only made of grass.

Our second letter today is from a Miss Gladys V., who writes:

For the past eight years I have been secretly engaged to a married man. My father thinks I have been going to a night class in glass-blowing. This man has told me over and over that his wife does not understand him and that he only loves me but since I have known him they have had five more kids and I am wondering if I am wasting my youth on a man who does not know his own mind.

The other night recently I told this man he would have to choose between me and his wife. He chose his wife. Do you think he is trying to shield me from something?

Dear Gladys V.,

You have certainly fooled the old man, but beyond that your tactics would hardly thrill General Ridgway. You should realize that it is usually a mistake for a girl of your type, that is to say daft, to go out with married men. Some men will exploit a guileless girl's devotion to their own ends, such as getting her to wash their socks or clean the furnace pipes. Don't let this happen to you, Gladys V. After eight years the man should know whether your liaison is just an idle whim or, as seems more likely, a very busy whim. Tell him to put his cards on the table the next time he makes love to you. Nobody can make love with a handful of cards.

And maybe you'd better tell your father about women.

A HELPING HAND

I WALKED through the wall, or at least where the wall will be when the carpenters are through re-modelling the office. (One school of thought says that the carpenters will never be through remodelling the office, but these are just soreheads who work in the rooms affected and can't see the funny side of putting on their hat and getting a collarful of saw-dust.)

The wall I walked through was just a skeleton of two-by-fours. It always amazes me the way carpenters can transform a few raw two-by-fours into a piece of gracious living. I know I couldn't do it. I've helped turn gracious living into a few raw two-by-fours, but anybody can do that by sambaing with a fat girl.

"What's this space going to be?" I asked one of the carpenters.

He didn't reply immediately. I've found that carpenters like to think out their answers, especially when they've got a mouthful of nails. The world would be a better place if diplomats were all car-penters with a mouthful of nails. (This is my thought for the day. If you know a better thought for the day, go to it.)

I watched the carpenter hammer in all the nails he had, and said:

"You're putting a wall through here, eh?"

60

He threw a fresh handful of nails into his mouth and renewed his hammering. That was the first intimation I had that some of the new construction in the office was top secret.

I have suspected for some time that some of the rooms in this office are closed to the public. I have seen the women members of the staff handing each other a key to one room. They never hand it to me. Then again the photographers have their dark rooms, where they lock themselves in for long periods and come out with crumbs on their mouth.

So I wasn't surprised to find the carpenter being tight-lipped about the wall. The man was just doing his duty. I didn't want to get him into trouble. I went away.

Having nothing pressing to do I went over and watched the electrician. The electrician was working with dozens of telephone wires strung all over the office. You would be astonished to see how many telephone wires a large metropolitan newspaper must have to answer people wanting to know what happened to the paper boy tonight.

"You've certainly got an awful bunch of wires there," I said to the electrician.

The electrician picked up a phone, said something into it I didn't hear and put it back. I guess those fellows get so used to using the phone that they lose the knack of talking to people in person. Watching him work with all those wires, though, I admired the way he knew which one was which. I would never have thought I could help him with a job like that, but after a moment or two he asked me to.

61

"You're in my light," he said.

By moving to one side I was able to let him see what he was doing. This gave me a sense of participation. It's good to work with your hands. It's even better to work with somebody else's hands. I went back to the carpenter, who had been joined by another carpenter, both looking out the window at a jeweller's clock across the street.

"It's ten to," one of them said.

"I've got five to," the other one said.

"The time?" I said eagerly, looking at my watch. "You're both a little fast, I think. I've got quarter to 12."

The carpenters both looked at me as though I was Management, a very severe look it was. They picked up their lunch buckets and walked away.

There didn't seem to be much point in hanging around, so I went to lunch too. I was hungry. That hammering and sawing can give a man quite an appetite, you know.

BIGAMY, ANYONE?

THE paper says we are having a wave of bigamists. It is interesting to consider what this may lead to, if bigamy becomes really popular.

Right now it leads to jail. But that is not because bigamy violates any fundamental moral law. The only reason bigamy is illegal is that if one man has two wives, another man has no wife. The outlawing of bigamy is just a measure men have taken to make sure they are not the little pig who had none.

There is nothing wrong with a man having two wives. It is only unfair, if there aren't enough women to go around. The growing numerical superiority of women, the depletion of males by recurrent wars, combined with the large body of bachelors and divorced abstainers, suggest that soon there may be enough women to go around. The question is, would they go?

I think they would. Naturally, a woman would prefer to have a man to herself. But, all other factors being equal, most women would, I think, prefer sharing a man to having no man at all. More than that, if polygamy were socially acceptable, most women would sooner share an exceptional man than own a clod outright. Women have an instinctive flair for what is best for the species. A man chooses a wife but a woman chooses a father for her children.

(A young lady once admitted to me, after our first date together, that she was already thinking about what our grandchildren would look like. It gave me quite a turn.)

Mother nature has no objection to the harem. If ducks are monogamous, a great many vertebrates generally considered to be higher than ducks—including the mighty elephant—keep the species strong by functioning as a herd. I don't wish to stress this point too much, since I have found that women usually resent woodsy parallels of this kind, but I think at least one of the dangers of monogamy is demonstrated by the Black Widow spider. She eats her husband. The American human male, already partially consumed, might well ponder the connubial practice of the Mormon.

If nature doesn't object to a plurality of wives, modern society would seem more and more to justify it. With the present degree of prosperity, many men are quite able to care for more than one wife. But more significant, an increasing number of women find themselves childless spinsters simply because they have devoted more time to making a career than to getting a man. These include some of the most intelligent women in our society, thoroughly capable of having bright, healthy children and carrying on their career at the same time. If a man could have two wives, say, would it not give greater variety to the species to have one child by each of them than two children by one? Must the other woman pay for her career with barrenness?

If this argument fails to satisfy women, including career women, it is not because of any moral qualms.

On the contrary, women reject it only because they have become accustomed to consider the husband as a wife's exclusive property. Property, Proudhon said, is theft. Thus the feminine insistence on monogamy is moral only if you consider competition and monopoly to be somehow sacred. Monogamous marriage is the ultimate expression of capitalism.

As a result, men who are born leaders of a herd of females must either pursue the supernumerary women out of wedlock, with undesirable consequences to all involved, or must sublimate the urge by dominating a herd of men, or a flock of dollars, as a tycoon, with even more distressing results. The man who can't acquire more wives will expend his energy acquiring more objects which which to bedeck the wife he's got. The sour expression on the face of the middle-aged American male proves that giving your wife a new roadster can never replace giving yourself a new redhead.

This is why I feel sorry to see a bigamist being sent to jail. He may have the key to the future, when everybody will be married to somebody, and the men will look tired but happy.

THE PLATTER OF BIG FEET

"A DELIBERATE attempt to undermine the morale of all the poor spinsters looking for husbands—not to mention the lonely widows!" writes a lady, referring to a news story about women's feet getting larger. She asks me to back up her contention that if modern woman has a big foot we should keep it under our hat.

I don't see how this thing can be hushed up. I have suspected for some time that women's feet were getting bigger, but I didn't want to say anything. It was up to the shoe people to blurt it out. They have the special equipment needed to measure a woman's foot.

The small, dainty foot of his mistress has always been worth a spasm or two from the poet. There is something appealing about a tiny trotter. It takes a woman out of the pelican class and puts her in with the deer and the antelope.

There should be no doubt, when a woman is ready for bed, whether she has remembered to take off her skis. When a man throws himself at a woman's feet, there should be at least some chance of his missing.

I can see where it could be discouraging for a spinster to spend a lifetime waiting for something to turn up, then find it was only her feet. But she

There is something appealing about a tiny trotter.

has the comfort of knowing that her feet are merely joining the trend to putting the stems in larger vases. Even the Japanese women have given up binding their feet, and Madame Butterfly will soon be snowshoeing around with the rest of us.

I have a theory about feet that might console somebody. My theory is that women with large feet are usually easy-going, loving and kind to dumb animals (men), whereas women with small, high-arched feet are often skittish and not particularly British. The same applies more or less to men, explaining why so few male ballet dancers are former members of the police force.

I admit that this is only a theory at the moment. All I know is, the woman with the smallest feet I ever became familiar with had a room full of photos of herself, while the woman with the largest feet I've known wanted a photo of *me*. You can't dismiss that kind of evidence. I hope to continue the investigation, however.

More obvious is the fact that women's feet are getting bigger because the whole body is going up like a balloon. Insurance companies never tire of telling us that our generation is several inches higher and wider than the last one. You can't stand a six-foot wench on a six-inch foot.

Thanks to improved diet and masses of vitamins we are getting bigger in everything except the brain, and in a thousand years or so we'll be larrumphing around like brontosaurus. To hear the patter of little feet you will have to be listening over the obstetrician's shoulder, and a severe earth tremour will be indistinguishable from Mother running for the bus.

The news of bigger-footed women is another hint that the goal of larger people is a dubious one. The world is over-populated, we know. Obviously, to save space and material, what we need is smaller people.

This is the most important idea I have had in some time. Since it may be even longer before I have another one, I shall repeat it: *We need smaller people.* Look how many ants can live in one ant-hill! Thousands of the little terrors, and the whole lot can keep going for months on the proceeds from one picnic.

The trick will be to reduce the size of the human frame without shrinking the brain, or at least its powers. I think four feet would be about the right height, just tall enough to be able to look a Great Dane in the eye. Pull this off, you bio-physicists, and the ladies will have back their lesser feet, food will be plentiful, and there'll be room in the bath for one more.

I have thought this out carefully, and believe me it doesn't sound as silly as it is.

HOW FAST IS TOO FAST?

THE news that the Air Force is having difficulty recruiting air crew is the most hopeful sign I've seen since that of the hamburger joint that opened up beside the dog pound.

The Air Force blames the thinning dribble of air crew on our young men's lack of enthusiasm for jet planes. The boys don't want to play. Splendid! Here is a hope for peace that nobody thought of, and I'd say it's worth at least five non-aggression pacts, 20 *ententes cordiaux* or 1,000 armistice talks.

Now, if Russia's youth would just show some reciprocal sign of distaste for the ghastly gadgets of war, we'd be away. They don't need to balk at jet planes, exactly. That would be a bit obvious. But they could fail to show up for the class in Skulking at the Spy School, or something.

As soon as we heard of it we could convert an aircraft carrier into a seashore pitch-and-putt. The minute we heard the Russians had followed this up with the announcement that their biological warfare branch was closed because of measles, we would push ten of our latest tanks off a cliff and send the Politburo a recording of the magnificent noise they made when they hit the bottom.

After that it would be a mad, hilarious carnival

of smashing bloop-guns and drowning destroyers, each side inviting the other to come over and tear the wings off a few bombers.

While we're waiting for the Russians to echo our apathy, I find it interesting to mull over this new restraint on the part of potential fliers. The young men, the Air Force says, are diffident about travelling faster than sound. They'd just as soon not. They're not fussy about the wide blue yonder if it means forfeiting the little old right here.

Now, *there's* a bug in the plans of the jet designer, risking his eraser on a blueprint. *There's* a fly in the ointment of the diplomat, flying nothing more supersonic than a swivel chair. *There's* a headache for the financier whose profits are kept up by a hurtling wing fused 'round some cloud-struck kid.

I am proud to say that I pioneered this distrust of airplanes. I didn't wait until they became jet-propelled. I became cool towards the airplane a matter of minutes after Orville Wright got it off the ground. It was probably my first pre-natal experience —a sharp feeling of suspicion about heavier-than-air flight. (I was also none too sanguine about lighter-than-air flight.)

This feeling was strengthened when I joined the R.C.A.F. during the war. The first time I took off, or rather was taken off, in an airplane, I knew that the whole idea was fundamentally wrong. The din of the engines, the ground racing by faster and faster, the aircraft straining to get off the ground, me flapping my arms crazily—it wasn't natural.

As soon as we landed and they told me I could open my eyes, I marched unsteadily to the orderly

71

room and told the senior corporal that the Air Force and I had made an awful mistake. We weren't meant for each other after all. I was sorry. I hoped we'd still be good friends. But I would have to ask to have my enlistment annulled.

What the corporal said does not concern us now. It's all lava under the bridge. I flew for the rest of the war, from time to time. I felt then and feel now that flying is for the birds. When compelled to fly these days, I still worry about the Duck.

My clear picture of the episode of the Duck builds before every take-off. Sometimes I see the Duck—it is an ordinary duck, minding its own business at about 5,000 feet—flying into the engine, sometimes flying into the cockpit and stunning the pilot, sometimes getting caught in the tail assembly and putting us into a quacking spin from which there is no recovery.

In the air, the Duck is as ineluctable as Destiny. On the ground he is a lovable clown. I prefer to meet him on the ground.

That's why I'm hoping that the reluctance of our young men to be fired out of a cannon, wearing a bit of fuselage and a wafer of wing, may herald that new age of physical cowards and mental valiants in which I shall feel so thoroughly at home, while the Duck flies undisturbed to his quiet grey marsh.

BACK-YARD BARBECUE

MY REJOICING in the coming of summer's sun is always modified by the knowledge that I must suffer the torture of the damned. Namely, roasting.

I don't tan. The sun doesn't transform me into a bronzed god. It turns me into a braised beet. Little Red Writhing Hood.

People tell me the sun does this because I am fair. That's what they say. What they mean is I'm the sort of thing that should only come out at night. Me and the dew worms. I know what they're thinking, blast them.

I wouldn't bother with the whole ugly business, except that these days everybody gets a tan. I see them on my way to the office, dozens of them, sprawled about Kitsilano Beach in their bathing suits, baking as much as the law will allow. I understand that even more of them go off into the hills and bake what the law *won't* allow, as well. These people may just want to look healthy, but they seem to me to go to unusual lengths to make sure that they will look well done from any angle. Anyhow, by midsummer all these people will be running around black as Othello, so that a Desdemona like me can't appear in public without being suffocated socially.

It's all very well saying that you have a fine white skin. Nobody wants to see a lily on thy brow these days. Thighs of alabaster are out. These days you're supposed to look like Aunt Jemima, if you have to carry a stack of pancakes to do it.

So, to avoid looking like something disturbed under a rotten log and running to save its eggs, I shall have to incinerate myself. Every year I try a different sun-tan lotion, something that my friends have told me will enable me to tan without burning. And every year I confront these friends, my little blue eyes glaring out of a boiled ham.

Olive oil was the thing, they told me. Complete protection. So I covered myself with olive oil, took a magazine into the back yard, lay down, and started reading about how the Italians do all their cooking with olive oil. I got up, went back into the house and washed off the olive oil. Nobody is going to catch me looking like an Italian entree.

Next I was persuaded to try a jar of a cream advertised by posters of a young woman pouting prettily over her third degree burns. She had dropped one strap of her bathing suit to show how white she was before she blundered into the sun without the cream.

The dropped shoulder strap was an inspired piece of advertising. I bought the cream. I smeared it over me like a Channel swimmer and waded stickily into the back yard. Lying on my back on some newspapers I quickly became a death trap for a large variety of bugs that became mired in the ventral ooze. The cream evidently made me smell like hollyhocks or something. A sizable insect of a species I didn't recognize tried to breast-stroke its way into the relative safety of my shorts. I got up and went into the house with the newspapers stuck to my back.

Since then I have tried several other lotions and creams. Some of them left me whiter than I was before I put them on, cleansing the pores, of all the dirty tricks. One made me brown but bumpy, and when the bumps went so did the brown.

Now I have resigned myself to peeling. I peel beautifully. If anybody wanted to make out a case for my having a dash of reptile in my make-up he'd only have to see me cast off my old skin and wiggle away gleaming in the new one. With me epidermis is no problem. I've got skin to burn.

And by the middle of September I'll begin to look almost brown. Then the sun will disappear and in two weeks I'll be shark's belly again. It hardly seems worth it.

Besides, the doctors say that excessive exposure to the sun is bad for the skin. I wish you'd speak up a little louder, doctors. These blighters don't seem to hear you.

MY UNPUBLISHED LOVE LETTERS

PUBLICATION of the love letters of Bernard Shaw and Mrs. Pat Campbell has reminded me of my own efforts to establish a literary romance.

It was right after the Thespian Society of Perth, Ontario, had performed my one-act play that I realized the time was ripe to start an incendiary correspondence. The task was not made easier by the fact that the girl I was squiring at the time lived only a few blocks down the street. It seemed like an awful waste of postage to write her letters. Besides she wasn't a famous actress. She worked in an office and just wanted to have babies. Obviously I had to look elsewhere.

I knew a girl in Toronto who wasn't exactly famous but who sometimes acted in Little Theatre plays, if they called for an idiot sister. It wasn't much, but it had to do. I wrote her a searing letter in triplicate, keeping one copy for my agent and one for myself.

"Cruel, cruel, heartless creature," I wrote, "have you forgotten so soon that night at Sunnyside Beach? You took my heart and flung it into Lake Ontario, and adulating cocker spaniel that I was I swam out and fetched it back for you to fling and fling again. Was it nothing to you that I loaned you my earmuffs, that day in the queue at the liquor store? O, thief of bliss, kidnapper of dreams, give me back my treasure.

"I have written a new play. It is very good. I'm aching to have you in it, but it is right that you should start with Shakespeare and work up.

"O, kitten, come to Papa.

E.P.N."

The letter came back marked "Not known at this address," with the cold command, "DO NOT REMAIL UNDER THIS COVER." Checking, I found that I had mailed the letter to the right girl but the wrong address.

It was a poor beginning, but I remailed the letter to the right address and sat back to wait for the epistles to start perking. Instead of a letter I got a phone call.

"Darling!" it said, "I've just got your letter. It's delicious."

"You shouldn't have phoned all the way from Toronto," I said hoarsely. "I was just—"

"Who's in Toronto?" I had almost forgotten that hyena laugh. "I've been in Vancouver for weeks. They forwarded your letter. When are we having dinner together?"

That one cost me a dinner, and I still had a file fresh out of passionate replies. I had to wait six months before another old flame went to England. As soon as she had landed I let her have it.

"My darling dearest tiger, tiger burning bright" —this sort of salutation is standard in literary love letters (c.f. Tchaikowski, "Letters to Madame Popoff," also Boswell's letters to practically anybody), and besides I couldn't remember whether her name was Marg or Marj—"you have gone away, the sun has set, darkness envelopes me. O Arctic night, so long, so cold, so icy-packed. When will Aurora gladden my sky again?

"My new play has been rejected by the CBC, a major triumph. Had the producer I showed it to accepted it I should have known that it was a miserable mediocrity. This is my fourth success in a row.

"Where are you my star, my galaxy, my whirling wondrous universe?

E."

I waited impatiently for two months. The time lapse in these exchanges is important, being a gauge of ardour in both parties, but I was prepared to alter the date on her letter if necessary. When the postcard came ("Here we are in Brighton. They have the longest pier here. Cornwall next! Bye-bye. Madge."), I tore up the date with the rest.

Since then my amorous correspondence with famous actresses has languished. Must get at it again. I wonder whether Margaret Rutherford would have time to . . .

HOME-TYPE HOLIDAY

I STAYED in Vancouver for my holiday this year and spent a lot of time arguing with people who said I should have gone away.

I don't think they just wanted to get rid of me. They felt that to spend a holiday in the comfort of home was sort of cheating. Some of them had spent their holidays at summer camp, toting that wood and lifting that pail, and they resented my evasion of these pitchy delights.

"A change is as good as a rest," they snarled, glaring out of eyes pinked by two weeks of tossing on a camp cot. "Get away from it all, for pete's sake."

My reply to this is that Vancouver is a summer resort. Thousands of people travel thousands of miles to spend their holiday here. Right now the city is full of folk from Toronto who have lugged the bags under their eyes out here to tan the leather in our gentle coastal sunshine. Why should I leave paradise just because it's handy? Who says a holiday should be trouble? Since when is relaxation something at the far end of a safari?

Of course one reason why hardship is such a popular part of a holiday is that it makes the return to work much more tolerable, even makes it a relief. Many people couldn't put up with their jobs if their holidays weren't charged with the old ghastly. A holiday points up the comforts of home, the desirable quality of one's own friends compared to the saw-toothed lot one meets at a summer resort, and the advantage of one's regular employment, even though it's labelling pickle bottles, over driving 200 miles across scorching desert with kids whimpering in the back seat and every motel offering the stark greeting: "No Vacancy."

Well, I've smartened up. This year I moved the lazy-boy chair into the back yard, in the shade of the old peach tree. I laid a good book on my stomach where I could reach it if the urge to read came over me irresistible-like. I closed my eyes and let the sun melt down the little knots of nerves.

If I felt more active, I had a choice of tennis, swimming, golf, hiking, fishing and eating. I chose eating. Good food served at cost.

Oh, I know that this sort of holiday wouldn't suit everybody. I know that many people, especially young women, deliberately get away from home so that they can make new acquaintances. There is something about a dude ranch or a beach resort that binds the guests together.

Sometimes it's the skimmed milk on the corn flakes. Or the crows that start their revival meeting every morning at 5 a.m. Plenty of girls have caught their future husbands in the simple trap of a summer resort lounge whose only other diversions are a broken phonograph and a small, battered library of books, the most exciting title of which is "100 Things to Make with Mud."

But I don't see that this is a holiday, exactly, any

more than the long motor trips from which father returns with his fingers frozen into claws from too much steering wheel, or the beach camps where mother sweats at keeping up steam in a wood stove whose smoke scorns the pipe and prefers to rough it through her lungs.

You can't tell me that kind of change is as good as a rest. This kind of holidayer is like the man who beat his head on the floor because it felt so good when he stopped.

Mind you I'm not saying that I succeeded in attaining Nirvana first try, on this holiday. The holy men of India do it by sitting contemplating their navels, but when I tried this I was merely reminded that I should cut down on the fats and starches. But if I didn't conquer the cosmic itch for a change, at least I wasn't scratching so hard. I just relaxed and enjoyed myself.

Guess that's why I don't feel as though I've had a holiday.

HOW AMERICA DISCOVERED COLUMBUS

TONIGHT I find myself (and not for the want of looking) fed up with routine and seriously thinking of becoming a missionary. You know any good places where a fellow could mission? The place should be warm, with a blue lagoon and plenty of convertible women.

You ever get to feeling like that? Okay, let's organize another Kon-tiki expedition. We'll call it Kin-toki and appoint each other full Kin-toki colonels. We then go to the West Indies and build a raft to prove that Columbus didn't discover America after all, but *America discovered Columbus* (italics mine).

My theory is that Columbus was a born landlubber and would never have set sail for anywhere if Isabella hadn't been forced to get him out of town. Well, as we know, Columbus had these three ships built, the *Ave Maria,* the *Esperanto* and the *Spadina.* Every day Columbus would exhort the shipbuilders to greater efforts, and every night he would sneak down and pull a few planks off the ships.

At last the ships were ready, however, and all preparations were completed for setting sail the moment Columbus could find his crew, and vice-versa. Isabella was finally obliged to employ a press gang, composed of three managing editors and a copy boy, who promised Columbus that if he would sail they would get him coverage on the front page of the court circular. At that time the court circular, a spicy tabloid called *Portu Gals,* had only one page (the front), but Columbus fell for it and the fleet set sail.

As soon as it was out of sight of the dock the fleet dropped anchor. Columbus was no fool. He had no itch to find a new route to India. He didn't even know the *old* route to India. As far as he knew, pepper came from the corner grocery. So he just parked the *Ave Maria,* the *Esperanto* and the *Spadina* in a circle and settled down to a quiet game of three-handed bridge.

Columbus figured on passing a couple of months this way, then sailing back into port and telling the Queen and her people that he had seen India and they wouldn't like it.

At this point, Fate took a hand (the *Esperanto* was dummy). For at this same time a group of Florida aborigines had built themselves a raft of cypress trees, having first stripped them of Esther Williams and her underwater ballet, and set sail east.

Thanks to the prevailing Trade Current (or Great Circle Route), the raft was carried out into the Atlantic, and thanks to another prevailing Trade Current it was carried back to Florida, so that the natives had the embarrassment of waving good-bye to their families all over again as they were carried past the coast and back into the Atlantic.

"Indians!" he cried.

Now, my theory is that this time they were struck by a storm which hurled them clear across to the coast of Portugal, so that one day Columbus looked up from a three-spade bid to see this handful of tattered, half-starved natives climbing over his clean rail.

"Indians!" he cried, and quickly ordered his ships to form a tight circle with the women and children in the middle.

While the women and children were splashing around and drowning and the inadequacy of Columbus' strategy was becoming apparent, one of the natives crept forward and placed a solid gold bidet at Columbus' feet.

I don't think I need to tell the rest of the story, even if I could think of it. History already knows how Columbus described this wonderful new land to Isabella, showed her the gold bidet and the natives that he said he had brought back from that far shore. Then he did the egg trick and became immortal.

All right, chaps, who's game to prove this theory of mine? We'll pack our lunches and make a day of it.

AUTUMN'S POP CONCERT

THESE MORNINGS I wake up to hear the harbour in labour. The season of fog is born.

"Mooooooooove!" warns an invisible freighter.

"Yipe!" says a tug.

"Slowwwwwww!"

The foghorn is taking a very dim view, groaning: "Tooooooooooo bad."

"Yipe!"

"Boo!" (A smart Aleck.)

"No! No! No! No!"

"Tooooooooooo bad."

The voices of autumn are with us again. All too soon the bassos of the Bay will be joined by the sharper tones of trolley buses and automobiles, by the Oxford-accented indignation of the English car at finding so many pedestrians walking on the sidewalk. (I am waiting to see how the trolley buses make out in fog. We used to follow the red light of the street car with confidence in the tracks, but a trolley bus could quite conceivably run right into Lost Lagoon, taking a daisy chain of cars with it. Fun!)

The sounds of autumn are mostly sad and low.

"Ugh," I said, when the garage man told me I needed a new battery.

"Duhh," I said, when he told me a new battery would cost me $20.

"Rowowowowow," moaned my starter, after I told the car I couldn't afford a new battery.

"Hummm," said the bank when I cashed a cheque for $20.

"Tooooooooo bad," sighed the foghorn.

On the dew-wet lawns the robins are gathering for the flight south, and singing sad ditties about the worms that got away. Their love songs are laid away 'till spring.

On the golf course golfers pause to listen to a gentle rain in the trees, the whisper of the first leaves falling and alerting the woods to winter. The golfers modulate their curses.

In the department stores the murmur has migrated from bathing suits to badminton rackets, from garden furniture to hot water bottles. In the shoe departments is heard the sharp intake of breath, as feet lose the pagan freedom of summer sandals to be crabbed into something as sturdy as a vice.

At the University another murmur begins, the drone of lectures, a soothing sound, a sound to sleep to after a hard summer of working in a forestry camp. And what is that slighter sound, that thumping when a pretty freshette and the senior football star catch each other's eye across the library table? Something wrong with the heating system? Very seasonal disturbance.

Wait. What is that heavier thumping? From the office of the president of the soft drink company. The manager wants to know why sales are dropping off just because the weather's getting cooler? Somebody has suggested that the answer to iced tea is hot pop?

The manager doesn't like it? Thump, thump, thump, the apples are falling off the tree next door.

Hark to that horny, hissing sound! That is the coal merchant rubbing his hands together. That is the chimney sweep, busy as Santa Claus. And, oh, listen closely, there is the spider's spinning a new web to replace the one you swore through going out this morning, in time for you to swear through it coming in tonight.

And so, as summer softens into fall, we hear the gentle sobbing of a hundred housewives shorn of their iceman, and the anticipatory sighs of a hundred more whose taste runs to plumbers.

That clicking noise? Yes, that one's seasonal too. That's the sound of newspaper columnists racking their brains for something new to say about the coming of autumn.

"Tooooooooo bad."

THE ENIGMA OF THE WOMAN DRIVER

I SEE that the Traffic Commission has been muttering about women drivers again. It has the vague feeling that women drivers are responsible for something or other, but it can't pin them down.

The woman driver has long been the butt of crude jests and male derision, none of which has been authenticated by established fact. First-hand studies have been impaired by the sudden death of the researcher.

I have made a few notes on the subject that may help clarify the situation.

First, I have noticed that women drivers hardly ever have a serious accident. I can't remember hearing of a fatality involving a woman driver. Women drivers have nearly all their accidents in the garage. Women find no challenge in driving into the garage without hitting the doors or knocking out the back end. It bores them.

But on the road women drivers have an immense maternal concern for human life. Unlike men, they don't take chances. They keep their car completely under control, usually by travelling at a steady 20 miles per hour. Normally if they cause a death it is not by collision but by apoplexy. A woman driver may often be seen heading a procession of cars driven by men with purple faces. When one of these men finally pulls out to pass the line of cars he meets another male driver coming from the opposite direction. The rending crash of metal is not even heard by the woman driver, proceeding serenely ahead. This is Classic Pattern A.

Women drivers have their own brand of hand signals. Some of these are:

(a) *The left hand extended horizontally:* the driver is toying with the idea of making a left turn, or possibly a right turn.

(b) *The left hand extended horizontally with the forefinger waggling:* the driver is tapping the ash off her cigarette.

(c) *The left hand extended horizontally, and moving backwards:* the driver is pointing out a dress sale to her companion.

(d) *The left hand extended horizontally, palm upward:* the driver is ascertaining whether she should step out of the car in her new hat.

(e) *The left hand extended horizontally, palm downward:* new engagement ring.

These are the standard hand signals for women drivers. It should be noted that the woman driver never uses the signal for coming to a stop. She prefers to slow down gradually, like the *Queen Mary*, often from about a half mile out. This puts her exact intentions in doubt and so fascinates other drivers that they knock down a pedestrian. This is Classic Pattern B.

As can be seen, the safest place on the road is in a car driven by a woman. The only time I ever felt nervous beside a woman driver was when I was parked with one at Second Beach, in a secluded spot behind some trees. That, however, was a special case (a redhead).

Downtown the woman driver is liable to take somewhat longer to park and depark than a man. It is not wise, if you are looking for a parking space, to stop and wait for what appears to be a woman pulling out. She may be pulling in. The jerking back and forth provides no conclusive evidence of what she is up to. By the time you find out you probably have a ticket for double parking. This is Classic Pattern C.

Certainly women drivers have better manners than men. They are not horn-happy. The road-hog is rarely a sow. A woman will give you the right of way whether she has it or not.

Also, I have never seen a woman driving with her arm around a man's neck. I can't even picture it. If any man has ever had this experience I don't want to know about it. I wish I hadn't even thought of it.

Anyhow, from this partial study I think it is apparent that women are not bad drivers. They are just *different* drivers, that's all. And it's too bad they had to come along just when we were already nervous about one thing and another.

CIRCUS NERVES

I WENT to the circus last night. It was a wonderful circus, but I didn't enjoy it. I worried too much.

I worried that the high wire artists would fall. I worried that the juggler would drop something. I worried that the elephants would drop something else. I worried about the trick cyclists, about the dog acts—even the clowns I worried about (I know how crushing it is to act silly and not get a laugh).

The circus performers all finished their turns without mishap and bounced away in fine fettle, but when I left I had gas. I had worried myself gaseous.

I should have known that a circus was no place for me. I am world's worst worrier, even in the most routine situations. Even in church I'll worry that the beadle or boodle or whoever he is will drop the collection plate. On the highway I drive everybody else's car as well as my own. A strapless evening gown puts me in a state of ecstatic misery. In fact life provides very few situations in which I can't get in a good lick of worrying.

The time I went up to the second platform of the Eiffel Tower I had to come right down again. A lady was leaning over the rail with her handbag in her hand. I worried that the handbag would slip, the lady would lunge after it, I would lunge after the lady, and in accordance with Galileo's Law of

Falling Bodies the handbag, the lady and I would hit the ground in that order.

At the play I am a major worry-wart. The curtain goes up, a maid enters carrying a tray covered with tea service, and right away I am all winced up for the crash. When I write my stage play, as I shall any year now, I shall make sure that in no scene does any of the actors serve tea, climb a tree, brandish firearms, eat an apple or toy with a letter opener. I would also like to rewrite *Hamlet* to cut out the dueling scene at the end, because when semi-professional companies do it I worry that somebody will get a semi-professional skewer in his mezzanine. I'd change it to a pillow fight.

By the same nervous token, ballet is ruined for me if the men's tights are too tight. When the lads come leaping out of the wings in a *grand jet* I'd be happier if they were wearing plus-fours. The women I don't worry about so much. You can't get into much trouble in one of those fluffy little skirts.

I don't know what term a psychiatrist would apply to my kind of worrying. As you can see, it's worrying about things that haven't happened, and to other people at that. Why should I worry that the concert violinist will get his nose caught in his bow? Let him get it caught, if he wants to! It's not my fiddle.

A lot of people don't suffer from any kind of worrying, otherwise there wouldn't be crowds at prizefights and auto races. You wouldn't find me dead at a prizefight or an auto race. I might look dead, but I'd just be worried stiff.

One thing I will say for the movies is that they

spare me this kind of mental nail-biting. If an actor knocks over a wall in a film (in "Samson and Delilah" for example) I can be reasonably certain that the script called for it, and the collapse wasn't just due to flimsy scenery.

Still, I wish I could get over this drawback to live entertainment. As it is nearly all the lines on my face are fretwork. And I may want to go to the circus again sometime, and really enjoy something besides the trained seals. Trained seals are so extrovert and low to the ground that nobody could worry about them, but can a person build a cultural life around trained seals? I must remember to worry about that.

TALKING DOWN THE CAT

"THIS being National Cat Week," I said to the Captain, "I suppose I should put in a plug for cats."

Captain Fracas is our cat. Or perhaps it would be more accurate to say that we are his people. The Captain is part Persian and part sawdust. He brings the sawdust up from the basement in his fur, since he uses the sawdust bin as his bathroom. He is very tidy about going to the bathroom, but not so tidy coming back. In fact he is a mess. He is why the living-room floor sometimes looks like the Last Chance Saloon.

The Captain is ten years old now, pretty senior for a cat. He's had time to learn English, which he speaks with a slight accent that he knows people find charming. I have a smattering of Felinese, but we find it easier to converse in my own language.

"Cats don't need plugging," yawned the Captain. "Cats can look after themselves."

"A lot of people don't like cats," I said.

"A lot of cats don't like people," he murmured. "But we haven't started a National Humans Week yet."

"What cats don't like people?" I demanded.

"The cougar, the panther, the leopard, the lion . . ."

The Captain is always dragging in his influential relatives like this. Almost as annoying as the sawdust.

"You wouldn't know," I said tartly, "but some cats need protection. Alley cats, for instance . . ."

"Rank socialism," he interrupted (another bad habit). "Survival of the fittest keeps the species strong," and he belched in the manner of Charles Laughton.

"Survival of the fittest!" I hooted. "You lie around on a soft rug all day, get fed the best grade liver, wear a fur coat that didn't cost you a penny, never do a stroke of work, and you talk about survival of the fittest!"

The Captain calmly licked a paw before replying. Then he said:

"If I am so useless, why do you keep me?"

"Well . . ." There had to be a reason. "You're a good-looking animal. And you have a lot of personality. You hand us some laughs."

"Exactly. The talents of a first-rate insurance salesman. A good salesman makes six or seven hundred a month. I get a couple of dollars' worth of liver, padded with that cheap cat food you buy." The Captain blinked. "Sometimes I envy the alley cat's integrity, but balancing on the rim of a garbage can is not my idea of the way to eat dinner."

"It's not just a matter of hardship," I said quickly, noticing that the Captain was beginning to doze. "Some people just can't stand any kind of cat. They hate cats. They prefer dogs, that are open and friendly and wag their tails because they are happy, not because they're sore."

"Escapists," murmured the Captain. "Need their ego bolstered. Dogs make people feel important and necessary. Cats make them feel like just another

96

mammal. Dogs make people feel that it's love that makes the world go round. Cats prove that it's fresh meat. We're bound to be unpopular with the romantics." His eyes closed, his chin nestled in his paws.

"In that case," I said with some asperity, "I shall not plug National Cat Week and alienate a section of my readers. I shall write about something else."

"You're not going to use that confounded type-writer!" cried the Captain, fully awake. He has sensitive eardrums.

"I certainly am," I crowed, sliding in a sheet of copy paper. "Like this."

I started banging away. Cursing, the Captain got up and went into the bedroom. I had beaten him again.

SORTIE TO SAN FRANCISCO

San francisco—Doodling en route to Hollywood:

To catch Great Northern train, am obliged to get up at 6.30 in the morning. Take one look at blackness outside, cancel trip and crawl back into bed.

Dragged out by mercenary relatives, who point me, walking in my sleep, towards the Great Northern station. At station, find I'm to have company of herd of Shriners on way to convention. Shriners divided into two groups—those wearing wicked, anticipatory grins and those accompanied by their wives.

Train no sooner in motion than am beset by U.S. customs and immigration officers. Having boarded train with clear conscience, by time we reach White Rock am wearing hunted look. Wonder whether I should confess having once gone for bike ride with Jack Coldwell, son of the CCF leader. Prepared to swear I have since given it up (biking). They let me through, but I know they're watching me.

At Blaine am struck by inscription on Peace Portal: "Children of a Common Mother." Makes Britannia sound like a bit of a tramp, surely. Obviously chosen for the rhythm of the line. "Children of the Same Mother" no good. How about

"God Bless Our Mom?" Must remember to write a letter to the editor.

By Seattle, Shriners are beginning to feel their oats (or is it rye?). One Shriner rushes down aisle with roll of toilet tissue, distributing pieces and crying, "Get your morning paper." Bless his dear pointed head.

Change trains at Seattle, losing Shriners and picking up infant with splendid pair of lungs. Pass sign beside track saying "Route of the Great Big Baked Potato." One more person in our coach and it becomes the Route of the Great Big Mashed Potato.

During lull in roar of wheels, small boy in front of me asks mother, who has just returned to seat:

"Where've you been, Ma?"

Mother murmurs something. Boy loudly:

"Wha'd you say, Ma?"

"I said I was in the washroom."

After short pause, boy asks in loud voice:

"What were you doing in the washroom?"

"Guess," snarls the mother.

"Were you brushing your teeth, Ma?"

"Yes, I was brushing my teeth."

Boy laughs, and yells: "YOU'RE BLUFFING, MA!"

Mother apparently strangles boy and train starts moving again. Incident confirms my theory that children are 99 and 44/100ths per cent. pure mischief.

Arriving in San Francisco for first time, am impressed by hazy, hilly splendour of the city seen from Oakland ferry. Not knowing location of my hotel, take yellow cab, whose driver asks: "Where is it?" Adds: "I only been on this job two days" and misses bus by a grey hair.

At hotel, manager is short of single rooms, so he gives me a room with twin beds. Life offers no sadder reminder of celibacy than to be given a hotel room with twin beds.

Have lunch in one of those vast American cafeterias where you have to watch your coat through field glasses.

"What do you want?" asks the fat lady behind the steam counter.

"What have you got?" I say.

"We've got a little bit of everything."

"I don't think I can afford a little bit of everything," I quip, crisp as lettuce, but fat lady remains deadpan. Obviously a great difference between Canadian and American sense of humour.

Rubber-necking happily, find streets of San Francisco full of soldiers with their pockets full of hands. Feel guilty as civilian. Frightening evidence of country bristling with military strength. Which came first, the soldier or the war?

Store sign: "Over a Mile of Counter for Your Shopping Pleasure" reminds me that feet are starting to curl. Cap the gape with a gander at San Francisco's Chinatown. Chinese writing the supreme test for neon signs, but at last the twain have met.

And so to beds.

TOO MANY PIGEONS

Vancouver has been having a good deal of trouble with its pigeons. Every city has trouble with its pigeons sooner or later. You allow one pigeon in and first thing you know you've got thousands of pigeons, bumming around the streets, desecrating the banks, and making those cooing noises outside your window that just mean more pigeons.

As always, the pigeon-struck city has split into two groups—those who would discourage the pigeons by killing them, and those who rush to the defence of pigeons, defying anybody to touch a feather of their head. The animal and bird lovers are very strong in Vancouver, and would undoubtedly defend the right of a full-grown rhinoceros to park on Granville street. So, the struggle is for the moment deadlocked.

One of the chief sufferers from the surfeit of pigeons, the Bank of Montreal at Carrall and Hastings, has set up a pair of stuffed owls on the cornice to frighten the pigeons away. These owls obviously can offer only temporary relief. The pigeons have merely moved up the street to the Bank of Commerce, and are in fact already edging back towards these owls that are suspiciously indifferent to weather and all calls of nature.

As a public service I have attempted to consider

These owls can offer only temporary relief.

the pigeon objectively, to decide whether it is more a boon or a nuisance. Somebody had to do it. We can't go on like this.

Well, first of all, aesthetically the pigeon doesn't, I think, dazzle one. It is not a very pretty bird. As a matter of fact it is a rather obscene-looking bird. Its feet are too red to be savoury, and it has a way of shooting out its neck like a nervous tout. It cannot be entirely by chance that the pigeon spends most of its time in the gutter. It must like it there. Also pigeons congregate in the most disreputable part of the city. You don't see them in the gutter in the better neighbourhoods. They hang around pool halls and beer parlours.

It is my personal opinion that pigeons have nasty minds. This opinion is based on an experience I had in a London lodging house, where pigeons kept peering in the window. They sneaked along the outside ledge and peered in. I don't know what they hoped to see, but I wouldn't put it past them. They had red rims around their eyes and an air of having seen everything and done everything. They made me nervous with this peeping tommery, then finished me off with the pistol crack of their wings when they flew away. I grew to dislike them intensely.

On the other hand, I am the first to admit that pigeons grace a public square. They give it life and animation. It would be difficult to imagine London's Trafalgar Square without its swirling veil of pigeons. Squared pigeons afford old gentlemen something to feed when they can't afford to feed anything else, and thereby make the old gentlemen feel useful and good. If it weren't for pigeons most of us would have no quotation from the works of Gertrude Stein, whose line "Pigeons on the grass, alas" captures something of the depressing effect of the bird when grounded.

In fact, what the pigeon controversy boils down to is that pigeons are, generally speaking, decorative in flight and repulsive on foot. It is a great pity that pigeons have to land. But the fact is that pigeons *do* land, and what is worse, having landed, they are in no hurry to take off again. Most Vancouver pigeons, especially the old panhandlers, can get out of the way of feet and tires with merely a short sprint and twist of the hips. Flying is too much like work. They'd sooner walk up and down in front of the bank, giving their impudent impersonation of the manager.

Everything considered, it is difficult to imagine why anybody would want a pigeon for a pet. Yet the country has its pigeon fanciers. Most of these pigeons are racing pigeons, or tumbler pigeons, however, the sort of clean-living, clean-thinking pigeons that have served their country in time of war by carrying messages. These pigeons are in the clear. Nobody wishes them any harm.

The pigeons that are causing all the trouble are those dubious characters with no fixed address that hang around the skid-road. These pigeons never carried a message in their life. They have no service record. The only shells they've ever seen are peanut.

Even so, we could not liquidate them without further justification. This, I'm afraid, we have. For, the symbol of communist propaganda throughout the world has become Picasso's dove of peace. And the dove, like the squab, is just a form of pigeon. In other words the pigeon is to say the least a fellow traveller. To this extent it is a menace to our democratic way of life. The pigeons' profanation of our banks and the statues of our leaders comes into focus as a deliberate type of sabotage. Those red feet take on a new meaning.

It is not for me to say what should be the fate of these feathered traitors. I have done my part, I hope, by presenting both sides of the case with complete fairness. I leave the final judgment to my betters.

THE CELLULOID LOGGER

WHENEVER I see a Hollywood movie about logging I wonder if I wasn't cheated in my own time in the woods.

The Hollywood logging camps all seem to be built around a pretty girl. Usually she is the superintendent's daughter, and we see her in the kitchen mixing a cake for the crew. We just know, from the capable way her lovely hands stir the dough in the little bowl, that it will be the fluffiest cake 600 men ever ate.

Now, when I was sent into the Malahat Logging Company operation at Port Renfrew, on the rugged west coast of Vancouver Island, I never saw a girl like that in camp. The only white woman in the vicinity was the foreman's wife, who never left the house on top of the hill, the one you had to climb 120 plank steps to reach. Cinematic love depends on the first, accidental meeting, and it is pretty hard to make a meeting look like an accident after you have climbed 120 steps.

The foreman's wife was the only decent woman for miles, and all the indecent women had been logged off years before. The Company wanted us to think about trees, trees, trees.

As a result, that camp was the quietest place I've ever lived in. Unlike the Hollywood logging camp, the foreman didn't slug it out with somebody every night. He was tired from a hard day's work, and he had those 120 steps to climb. Everybody was too tired after nine hours of falling, bucking, loading, track-laying, cold-decking, scaling, saw-filing, flunkeying or whatever the job was, to indulge in those peculiar screen brawls that leave the hero with only a becoming bruise on the cheek.

Of course, we didn't have any balsa-wood chairs, such as movie loggers use for hitting each other over the head with exhilarating effect. We didn't have any chairs at all. Plans for the *derrière* didn't go beyond the cookhouse bench and the bunkhouse cot. We didn't have the comforts of homicide.

Another unusual thing about those Hollywood loggers is that they hardly ever spit. I suppose the film makers feel that it might weaken a love scene between the foreman and the pretty girl if he had to get up in the middle of it, go lift the lid off the stove and spit into the fire.

I guess that's what I admire most about the movie loggers—their ability to hold their juice. We had a superintendent (called "the Push") who could hold his tobacco juice longer than any other man in the camp. I'm not saying that's why he got to be superintendent, but I know the crew had a lot of respect for him. He got special training in holding his snoose juice because his wife, who lived at the lower camp, took a strip off him if she caught him chewing.

So he had this power of holding his face absolutely immobile for up to five minutes at a time. The effort cost him an unhappy expression, though, a sort of pained look, and when he came around I worked extra hard, thinking something was wrong with the business, until I found out that was how a man looked when he had spent years fighting off a spit.

The heroes of the Hollywood forest can outstay even the Push, though, going through a whole picture without once betraying the wad tucked under their lip. Those fellows earn their money, all right.

Then again, I never met any loggers who felt the Romance of the Big Timber. The Romance of the Big Timber seems to be felt mostly by script-writers of the National Film Board, who plan those shots of logs splashing into the booming ground, and then go back to Ottawa. Most of the loggers I saw were out to get the forest before it got them. They didn't go to work with a song on their lips. If there was anything on their lips it was maple syrup.

All in all, if somebody were to make a film to catch the real personality of a west coast logging camp, it would best be a silent picture. Loggers live a life of action, with death lurking in every snag. They don't talk much. I got a reputation for being gabby because I said "Please" asking others to pass the butter. When loggers do talk, their English is of the earth earthy, with a dash of earth.

Such talking as the crew did at the Malahat, in the bunkhouses after dinner, was in various national languages. The Swedes got together around one stove, the Ukrainians around another, the Ontarians around another, and so on. Working my way through college at the time, I was speaking sophomore English. Nobody else in camp spoke my language.

108

I had to go down to the ravine and watch the bears eat the garbage.

No, I don't think Hollywood will ever capture the spirit of a Canadian logging camp. Where men are men the most important thing in life is food. It isn't easy to get dramatic conflict out of a stack of hotcakes. Good food keeps a logger happy while he's getting "stakey." What happens to the stakey logger when he hits town is dramatic, in a blurred sort of way, but perhaps too functional for real art.

There's drama in the logging camp, but it's much more subtle than anything hacked out by a scenario writer who has to arrange to have a smudged and decoratively torn starlet trapped in a forest fire. Although I spent only a few months at the Malahat Logging Company's camp, I gained some inkling of how, for instance, one's values can change. As the weeks went by, the fat old squaw who waddled around the lower camp began to look more and more like Rita Rayworth. *That's* something they have yet to put on film.

COLD FEET CURED

WELL, here it is the middle of October, time to start thinking about how we're going to keep our feet warm in bed this winter.

Any night now we're going to jump into bed, cry "Hallelujah!" and jump right out again. It'll be cold in there. Especially at the bottom. The bottom of the bed is where the cold bunches up and waits for a pair of unsuspecting feet to blunder into the trap.

I have already received one foot-warming suggestion from a reader, Mr. F. W. Heppenstall, R.N., of Lynn Valley. Mr. Heppenstall writes: "You can sleep warm by breathing through a piece of rubber tubing placed amongst the feet."

Before passing this suggestion on to you I thought I had better try it myself. I regret to say that though the feet prospered I had disturbing dreams of trying to siphon Burrard Inlet into a bucket. If this sort of dream is an improvement over the ones you've been having you might care to give Mr. Heppenstall's footnote a whirl.

The hot-water bottle I don't like, owing to a traumatic experience I had with a hot-water bottle as a child. The hot-water bottle waited until I was asleep one night, then unscrewed its stopper, so that I woke up suddenly in a lake. Like stout Cortez, I was filled with a wild surmise, encountering this in-board Pacific. I have been leary of hot-water bottles since. If they can't burn you or drown you they will leave their cold clammy bodies where your feet will find them in the morning. I don't recommend them.

But a wife is a useful rig. Or a husband. People with cold feet usually marry people with warm backs. A lot of warm-backed people think they have won a mate by their intelligence or beauty, never knowing that their main attraction is that of being a warm object that won't leak. This is fitting and right, since the old adage "cold hand, warm heart" also applies to feet, and the parky-pedalled type is usually very loving once you get its feet out of your stomach, so they tell me.

If you don't want to go that high, bed socks are a good idea. There seems to be some prejudice against bed socks, as being unmanly or something. We Canadians are afraid of bed socks because the house might catch fire and we'd run out into the street and people would see that we slept in Argyles, almost as bad as sleeping in sin. This is a pity, because putting on a pair of bed socks that have been toasted in front of the fire and then piling into bed is one of life's more luxurious experiences.

Bed socks are especially helpful if you are a kicky sleeper. If you kick the bed-clothes out from under the mattress, exposing the feet (or if you sleep in a short bed), bed socks can often make the difference between waking up with feet and waking up with a couple of frozen haddock.

Still another cure for cold dogs is a big fat cat.

111

The procedure here is, about a half hour before retiring, to take the cat, warmed by the fire, and put him on the bottom of the bed. When you are ready to climb in, you remove the cat and slide your feet into the place the cat has warmed with his body. You may feel that this is rough on the cat. Don't waste your sympathy. If he is anything like our cat he will wait until you have dropped off to sleep, then jump back on your feet and keep you awake while he washes himself and plucks cat harp music out of the coverlet. Kicking at the cat usually dislodges the bedclothes and you're right back where you started. I don't know why I mentioned it.

You notice that I have ignored the thermostatic-bedroom, electric-blanket crowd who can get into bed and be sure of finding it warm, rain or shine. These people don't know the meaning of cold feet, sleep in twin beds and get divorced at a frightening rate. Their problem, like their wiring, is more complicated. Some other time, maybe.

THE SCARS OF WAR

COPY of a letter to the director of veterans' pensions, Ottawa:

Dear Santa:

Having heard that you are paying veterans a dollar for every day spent as a POW, I hereby submit my claim for $365.

This will cover the year I spent as a prisoner at Mrs. Tooley's place in Ottawa.

I suffered cruelty at Mrs. Tooley's place because there were no other rooms in Ottawa and her husband played the violin. Mr. Tooley, or rather Major Tooley, was in the dental corps. You could tell this from the way he played the violin, because it set your teeth on edge.

Major Tooley played the violin in the room next to mine, the one I was renting, and he played at odd hours. He got up in the middle of the night and let fly with Paganini. Evidently he had trouble sleeping. So did I.

Major Tooley liked to play lively, difficult pieces. I guess he was trying to get something out of his system. Sometimes he'd try for an hour and a half before giving up. He'd go back to bed and I'd lie in mine, my wide red eyes staring at the ceiling.

Because Major Tooley was a major and I was a sergeant we kept different hours, so that I never saw

I guess he was trying to get something out of his system.

him once during the year I rented the room. Mrs. Tooley took my money every month. I never had the heart to tell her I was leaving because her husband made a violin sound as though the strings were still attached to the cat. Besides, there was no place else to go.

A large, pleasant blonde, Mrs. Tooley wanted somebody to mother. She pinched my dirty socks out of my bureau, washed and darned them, and sneaked them back in again. I'd open a drawer expecting to find the dirty shirt I'd taken off the previous day, and there, washed and ironed, would be the pair of pyjamas that disappeared the week before. A sudden burst of fiddle on top of this and I was ready to believe I was shacked up with a couple of leprechauns.

When I had been posted to Ottawa, with living-out privileges, I had thought that I had the war by the tail. But after a few weeks of Major Tooley's fiddle I was thinking back with longing to the barracks of Alliford Bay, where you were lulled to sleep by the sound of frustrated air gunners chopping holes in the walls.

One night, with Rimski-Korsakov coming loud and clear through the pillow over my head, I wondered whether the punishment for striking an officer held if we were both in our pyjamas at the time. I gave up the idea anyhow, not being sure that he didn't play the fiddle with his forage cap on.

About this time I became interested in the waitress at the Honey Dew. Olga was a very high blonde. Something about the way she gave me my pot of marmalade told me we were made for each other. A giggle later I had a date for the evening.

When I called for Olga her first question was: "What's your religion?" I suggested that the best place to discuss theology would be my room. Although Mrs. Tooley had never stipulated that I shouldn't take women to my room, she had never made, so to speak, a blanket invitation. I, therefore, asked Olga to join me in a stealthy approach, for reasons of security.

The front door squealed treacherously, and I lost a few pounds on the hall carpet, but I managed to propel Olga into my room without arousing the natives. In a matter of minutes we had disposed of religion as a topic, and I was coming in on the scarlet beam of Olga's lips, when suddenly the room rocked with "The Flight of the Bumblebee."

Olga apparently took this as a sign, and I recognized the rigours of romance paced to the bumbling bee next door. I was obliged to escort Olga from the premises.

"I've left my scarf in your room," Olga said, but I steered her firmly to a movie theatre and saw her home early.

When I returned to my room, Olga's scarf was gone, replaced by a pile of clean socks. I went to bed in a cold sweat.

Shortly afterwards I was posted back to barracks. But for months I would wake up panting, hearing fiddles, and to this day I can't listen to Heifetz or Menuhin without wondering if somebody is frisking my bureau for dirty linen.

I'll take the $365 in small bills, thanks.

TRUE OR FALSE

SOME weeks ago I read an ad for the latest aid to feminine beauty—pneumatic falsies, that is a bra that blows up.

I have waited patiently for this latest facet of inflation to be denounced from the pulpit, but our ministers apparently are afraid to touch it. I can't say that I blame them.

If, then, this is a lay subject, I feel I must give voice to protest. This department is dedicated to war on all that is false, especially if this department is likely to be the one to get fooled.

I think I am speaking for millions of men when I say that falsies are unfair. According to a recent survey, made by heaven knows what exhausted surveyor, more than fifty per cent. of the women in North America now wear falsies. This means that men can no longer trust their eyes. Unfortunately for the state of the general morality, what they *can* trust is not their ears.

Do I hear some lady, very anonymous, protesting that falsies are but an extension of the corset, the bustle, the high heel, the lipstick and the other accepted razzle-dazzle of feminine bewitchery? This is an interesting question and I'm glad I asked it.

My answer is that men enjoy an illusion but not a delusion. A man can delight in the added grace high heels and nylons give to a woman's legs without believing that she just naturally walks on her toes and has seams in her legs. He inhales a woman's perfume happily but not under the impression that her pores yield Chanel No. 5. He kisses her knowing that he will come out of the clinch tasting Midnight Pink and looking like a Paris chorus boy.

But how can he pin his faith on a sweater that is liable to puncture?

My feeling is that this time the ladies have gone too far. I know that they have been going too far since Eve ran up a hem on a figleaf, but this time they have gone too far for *me*. Maybe I'm quaint, I don't know.

All I know is, a woman whose physical charms prove to comprise mostly platform soles, padded hips, falsies, make-up and twelve-hour curls is putting a devil of a lot of weight on our common interest in good music.

My indictment of falsies includes the reasonable assumption that women endowed by nature rather than by the lingerie counter will tend to prove it. Already some peek-a-boo blouses are giving more boo per peek. Plunging necklines are likely to take one last plunge and never come up. Falsies will only encourage more revealing clothes, which . . . (Sorry, men, I seem to be off on the wrong tack.)

They're deceitful, that's what they are. They are like the Chief of Police's ghost cars. They are used in the belief that the end justifies the means. But whereas we can establish a code of means, ends remain a matter of opinion, so that any society that puts ends before means is buying itself a slice of chaos.

I hope I have made myself clear. I don't want anybody writing to the editor saying that I am a liar because he happens to know that the Chief of Police does not wear falsies. This is a serious matter, if you think about it, and I hope everybody has caught the overtones. If not, there are some more overtones on page 183.

As for the pneumatic falsies, I shall merely recount the true incident, relayed by a friend, of the high blonde who boarded a plane and took every male passenger's mind off the plane's take-off, thanks to her superb superstructure. But the plane had scarcely climbed into the sky before a choked cry was heard, and passengers turned to see the blonde purpling as changing air pressure made her chest expand in all directions. Quick action by the stewardess and a safety pin saved the victim, but the loud sigh of air heard was not one of male longing.

A word to the wise, fair maiden?

ICE-BREAKING MADE EASY

So YOU'RE going to have a party. And you're sitting there in a fine spray of bitten fingernails, worrying about how to break the ice that for some mysterious, Arctic reason always forms over your soirées.

Your skin still creeps at the memory of the *last* party you had, when everybody, including Miss Jones, rose at midnight as though propelled by a common catapult, saying they had to drive the baby-sitter home. Miss Jones must have been pretty desperate to grab at such an unflattering excuse. The girl panicked. You were lucky there wasn't an ugly pile-up at the door.

This time you are going to make sure that your guests don't sit around clutching their drinks like street car stanchions and looking as though they expect the ride to get rougher. People are going to have *fun!* If you have to break somebody's leg they're going to stay till 1 a.m.

Now, then, what are the best ways of making sure you are not playing host to a gallery of Sumerian stone idols?

First, the introductions. Right here is where the first thin film of ice starts forming. People get so tensed up trying to remember their own name while they forget everybody else's that you can hear the click of the refrigerator cutting in. Nor does it help to funk the introductions completely and let the guests introduce themselves. The men will all get to know the name of one woman (the one in the strapless evening gown), and the rest of the women will sit around thinking up new names for you.

One jolly way to handle introductions is to hang a large placard around each guest's neck as he arrives, a card bearing his name and occupation, if any. This placard will simplify the problem and also help cover what the strapless evening gown doesn't.

You will have found that, after the introductions, the most critical period of a party is the first hour. During the first hour the bashful, who always arrive early, keep rising and sinking to offer others their seat, while the drinkers who had hoped for straight rye are still sullenly getting used to your cocktails. In this period will occur those paralyzing silences when the whole assembly seizes up on you. The first time this happens, step smiling into the centre of the room and say:

"Well, now, would you like to see some colour slides of our trip to Smith Falls?"—pausing to let the full horror of this seep in, then adding, "Or would you sooner just talk?"

Any normal group of guests will start talking right away, almost hysterically, and won't give you a chance to get a word in edgewise for the rest of the evening.

Your next problem is to prevent splinter parties from forming in the kitchen, the basement and in extreme cases the bathroom. Guests always try to swim upstream towards the source of the liquor.

This can be frustrated by putting the liquor in your bodice, or by carrying it on your head in an urn.

About 11.45 comes the last crucial stanza of your brawl. Some of the guests have lapsed into bemused silence, smiling at something in the bottom of their glass: they are getting plastered. The girl who has failed to attract anybody with her attempt to look inscrutable is about to get up and declare loudly that she had better get home before the fog gets worse. The whole party is waiting to be shifted into high. So you let out the clutch and shout, "Game, everyone!"

What sort of game you play will depend on whether you just want to break the ice or turn it into live steam. In any event, the choosing of sides, a process that often allows the nimble guest to nip under a bed someplace, is expedited by the numbers on the backs of the placards everybody is wearing, or was wearing, blast them.

After a round of Charades or Spin the Bottle your party will be so well integrated that when you give the nod to the pianist the guests will move in a solid cluster to the piano, to fill the night air with sentimental bellowings. When the telephone starts ringing you'll know you've got a successful party on your hands.

It says here.

MAYBE IT'S JUST ME

One of the larger slick magazines is running another series of funny baby pictures. At least, they are presumably funny to somebody. They aren't funny to me.

I don't know when I stopped thinking that candid camera shots of babies were funny, but it was quite some time ago. I think the whole business started with photos of babies used to advertise talcum. Now it is almost impossible to open a magazine without finding huge shots of infants goggling, leering, drooling or otherwise carrying on in the nude. Such pictures apparently stop the woman reader dead in her tracks. "Ho, isn't that cute?" says the woman reader. The answer is "No." I require no pictorial evidence that people are still having babies, and that babies are capable of grotesque expressions, and that advertising agencies have no scruples about exploiting the female's urge to procreate. If I wish to be reminded of the fertility of the species I need only attempt to step into a street car at rush hour. These chubby memos in the magazines merely depress me before I can even reach the reading matter.

In that happier era before the perfection of the camera, photography was restricted to subjects that could keep still. This eliminated all but the reasonably adult and a few static children who looked to have been stuffed. That, as far as I am concerned, was the golden age of photography. Babies, irresponsible and fidgety, were quite rightly left out of the picture, or appeared only as a shapeless bundle in their mother's arms.

Then they built a camera that could freeze a drop of water in flight. After you've seen one drop of water frozen in flight you've seen them all, but this same camera will catch a baby in mid-grimace, so that we now have herds of photographers crawling around cribs, snapping thousands of pictures of babies on the chance of getting one photo in which the child looks anything but gormless.

This in turn has encouraged millions of amateur photographers who also happen to be parents to mug the fruit of their union every time it shows some sign of becoming a human being. The camera fiend who is also a new father represents the ugliest combination of enthusiasms since the more poisonous Medicis. Some fool has made movie cameras cheap enough for a lot of these fathers to get hold of one, and anybody who has sat through an evening of home movies based on the damp day of little slobberlips knows the meaning of justifiable homicide.

This sort of pictorial purgatory is, I submit, encouraged and intensified by the baby pictures that editors print in newspapers and magazines. What this movement back to the diaper means in terms of sociology I have no idea. All I know is, until fairly recently public display of babies was not considered to be in particularly good taste. In the better-run families, an infant was consigned at birth to a

124

nanny, and was not again brought into the father's presence until it was about six and able to say something intelligent. Neither the baby nor photographic proof of its manic depressive tendencies was considered to be of interest to visitors. Men didn't talk about such things, let alone permit the progeny to chuck its blocks at guests. Youth must be served, perhaps, but not before it has learned to hold its porridge.

If I were a baby, which I am increasingly not, I doubt that I would be grateful to my parents for the type of notoriety attendant to publication of a funny photo of me. Not all these tots can be orphans. Some of them at least must have parents who are milking junior's dimples for every sou they can get. Some of these babies look hopped-up to me. And at least one that I've seen I swear was a midget. The photo showed him naked only from the waist up, and with every reason in the world.

Look, what's wrong with photos of *old* people? Old people have character in their faces—good character, bad character, but character. A lifetime of living has etched its pattern on the faces of the elderly. They are worth studying. The great portrait painters gave us adults, not sucklings. And what ever become of the old-fashioned death mask? We seem to be keeping a man's record at the wrong end.

Well, I take the liberty of warning the editors that if they spread this epidemic of baby pictures there may be a reaction against babies. We won't care about baby's thin, sensitive skin if baby starts getting under ours. I refer the editors to a scene in a film called "Sitting Pretty," in which Clifton

Webb, in a fit of exasperation, clapped a bowl of mush over the head of the occupant of a high-chair. It was without a doubt one of the most satisfying scenes ever filmed. The glee with which audiences have received it may well signal the turning of the tide against toddlers. Speaking for myself, I shall be content when any interesting photos of babes I encounter will reveal those somewhat older children of the opposite sex. Photography must respect the true values.

THIEVING RAFFLES

ANYBODY know how to make a delicious Christmas dinner out of old turkey raffle tickets?

That's what we've got at our house. No turkey. Just raffle tickets. Big raffle tickets, little raffle tickets, blue ones, red ones, yellow ones. My wallet is full of them. No money. Just raffle tickets.

The turkey raffle tickets cost more this year, too.

Two bits each, some of them. This year we paid more for the turkey we don't get to eat than we paid for the turkey we didn't get to eat last year. Never before have so few paid so much for sweet nothing at all.

I've had a book of raffle tickets to sell at a dime each. Every time I put the bite on somebody he bites back with his tickets at a quarter each. And some of those boys are awfully fast on the Christmas draw. I'm still reaching for my raffle book when they have theirs whipped out and are wetting the point of their pencil on my tongue.

For many years I have bought my turkey raffle tickets according to a system. The system is infallible. It never wins.

Sometimes I buy the last ticket in the book. Sometimes I buy a ticket with a number whose figures add up to three, the way I add. Once I bought a ticket from a girl because *she* had a nice round figure. That one cost me plenty before I was through. I could have bought a whole turkey farm with the big fat upshot of that raffle ticket.

Anyhow none of these devices works. The turkey is always won by some playboy who didn't even consult his astrological chart before making the investment.

Some people are born lucky. They usually look like Bing Crosby, have a golf handicap of four and are married to a lovely woman who has given them two children—a boy and a girl.

I am not one of these people. It was while I was bending over to pick up a pin that I was hit by that dolly in the department store. I have had to work for everything I've got. This situation seems even more poignant when I realize that I haven't got anything.

But to get back to the turkey raffle tickets. I remember we did win once. That was about fifteen years ago, and we won two turkeys for the same Christmas. Instead of Lady Luck's smiling on us regularly, she turned around for this one belly-laugh.

That wouldn't have been so bad if one of the turkeys hadn't weighed about forty pounds. We tried to invite some people to help us eat the thing, but we'd won it too late. Everybody had made plans for Christmas. So there we were, my mother and my father and I, with this huge bird lying naked in the kitchen like Edward Arnold.

We found we didn't have a pan large enough to hold the turkey, so we bought a new pan. Once we got the turkey into the pan we found it wouldn't go into the oven. The top of the oven caught the turkey a good two inches below the crest of the breast bone, so for a while there it looked as though we might have to build a fire in the bathtub.

I think we finally got the turkey in by laying it on its side. Or maybe it was by laying the stove on its side. Anyway, we cooked it and stuffed ourselves with it and on Boxing Day it still looked in better shape than any member of the family.

That turkey was around so long we grew to hate all forms of bird life. After the first week Mother didn't even bother trying to camouflage it as chicken à la king or Irish stew. We just tore at the great carcass in cold fury, uttering low, inhuman cries.

I forget what happened to the second turkey.

Well, that has never happened again. This year we have had to buy a wild duck for Christmas dinner. It isn't really a wild duck. Actually it's a tame duck that went mad with hunger. We found it hanging in the butcher shop with a note beside it explaining why it did it. "Life isn't all it's quacked up to be," the duck had written.

Some of you people won't believe that was what the duck wrote and will say I just made it up. These are the same people that don't believe in Santa Claus. There are too many cynics in the world, and too many turkey raffle tickets. I'd like to see anybody disprove that.

DON'T JUST STAND THERE

EVERY article about Vancouver mentions that you can swim at a fine bathing beach and half an hour later be skiing up the mountain.

My pride in this remarkable civic achievement has always been nagged by the fact that I can neither swim nor ski. The things I do (eating, sleeping, swearing, etc.) I could do just as well in Big Muddy, Saskatchewan. For years I have felt like a traitor to my environment, and when people asked me if I swam or skied I have had to give them an evasive answer, such as "Yes."

Last summer I decided to learn to swim and to ski. It was too late in the season to learn to swim, but I got busy telling everybody I was going to learn to ski this winter. I talked this up so much during the fall that by the beginning of the year I felt I *had* skied, and I became critical of the other skiers I saw, in the newsreels.

But a couple of weeks ago at the Badminton Club, when I was enjoying the glow of well-being that always followed my telling somebody I was going to learn to ski, George, one of my audience, said:

"How about coming up Hollyburn with me Wednesday?"

I may have flinched a bit, but months of ski

talk had given me a certain verbal agility, and I was able to reply smoothly:

"Well, that sounds like fun, George. Unfortunately I haven't any skis, otherwise—"

"I can lend you skis," George said.

"I haven't any boots," I said "Otherwise—"

"I can lend you boots, everything you need," George said.

Livid at the monstrous generosity of the man, who after all barely knew me, I attacked his qualifications.

"I didn't know you could ski, George," I said.

"I'm an instructor for *The Daily Province* ski classes," he said.

That night I went home from badminton feeling much more tired than usual.

The next Wednesday morning it was raining. I phoned George.

"Raining, George," I said. "Rotten day for skiing, I guess, eh?"

"That's right. Next Wednesday then, okay?"

The next Wednesday brought a fine, horrible, sunny morning. George picked me up in his car and we drove to the base of the Hollyburn ski lift. He handed me my skis, which looked much lighter when he was carrying them, and we joined the cluster of skiers waiting for chairs.

When my turn came, instead of a chair whirling around the platform there came a sort of open-ended basket. George held me back, saying:

"That one's for the stretcher cases."

I caught the chair behind the empty stretcher basket, which preceded me slowly and confidently

131

up the hill. Swinging 20 to 30 feet above jagged stumps, the sky-hung tumbril gave me plenty of time to brood about the blind confidence people put in mechanical engineers.

"Look at the view of the city," George shouted behind me.

Turning, I saw a magnificent panorama of the city I had been fool enough to leave. I could pick out the General Hospital very easily. I turned back and found a man waiting to catch me.

In the handsome lodge I put on the ski boots, and a *Province* photographer who happened to be up looking for funny pictures suggested he take one of me lying on my back with my skis in the air. I said I didn't want my picture taken like that, so we went out to the snow, George put on my skis, I tried to move, fell on my back with my skis in the air, and the photographer took my picture.

A few attempts to keep my balance on the skis persuaded me that if skiing wasn't harder than I had thought the snow certainly was.

After I had fallen enough times to satisfy everybody around that needed a good laugh, George and I took off our skis for the hike to the Hollyburn Ski Lodge, where his class was waiting. His class was all women. The hills swarmed with women, swooping about and hammering a few more nails into the coffin of the expression "weaker sex."

Having experienced some difficulty in getting up on skis once my enormous weight hit the snow, I declined to provide burlesque comedy for a bunch of refrigerated Amazons. I retired to the cozy interior

The hills swarmed with women.

of the lodge, supplementing the group of fair, bronzed athletes with my pouchy pallor.

The young lady who gave me my coffee, with the friendliness of the fraternity said:

"There's one thing about skiing, you're never too old to learn. We have ladies of sixty up here skiing."

I said: "Uh-huh," and made a mental note to hate ladies of sixty.

As George and I started back down the trail, my legs rubbering puckishly, I took a last look at the snowy splendour of the mountainside, breathed in the deep silence that was broken only by the squeak of my vertebrae, and swore to speak of learning to swim to none but the heaviest anchors.

CARNIVAL IN KENSINGTON

AND a happy New Year to you, too.

Shall we, at this time, look back over the old year and pick out the highlights? Okay, you take the first six months and I'll take the last six months and as soon as anybody finds a highlight, sing out.

No highlight was the New Year's Eve party I went to last year. It was a party of upper-class English people in London. Never mind how I weaseled into a party of upper-class English people. In austerity-stricken London you could get into any place if you had an independent source of raisins. At that time I was loaded with raisins.

I like and admire the English people, but few sights are sadder, I found, than that of a group of public-school Britishers who don't know each other too well, assembled for an occasion whose chief requisite is revelry.

They are all longing to revel, but nobody wants to start it. The young gentlemen, hair parted sharply down the middle, stand around at acute angles, hanging onto their drinks as though they expect the rug to be pulled out from under their feet at any moment.

Talk is carried on in hushed tones about neutral topics, and you instinctively step around the invisible casket in the centre of the room.

Last New Year's Eve, when I walked into the Kensington drawing-room where a party was almost in progress, the murmur of conversation died and I caught people shooting glances at my jacket. I was wearing a dark red corduroy jacket with matching tie and raisins. Every other man in the room was wearing a black suit, except a few young sports in blue serge.

In Canada the red jacket had never caused the slightest quiver. In Kensington I felt like fireworks at a funeral.

A lieutenant-colonel whom I had already met sprang into the breach. The English are superb at springing into breaches. He came over to me and said distinctly:

"Say, that's a jolly fine jacket."

The tension was eased. The lieutenant-colonel had sacrificed himself for the party and for me. Through no fault of his own he knew me; and when an English gentleman knows you he will rally to your side even though you come in dressed as a rainbow with a pot of gold at your end. You can't beat a people like that.

I slunk into an obscure corner until midnight, when the hostess suddenly accused me of being the darkest man in the room. She told me I had to go outside and come in carrying a chunk of coal and ringing a small bell.

I took the coal and the bell and stood outside wondering what fine old English custom I was about to louse up.

At midnight I barged into the room brandishing the coal and ringing the bell, bellowing "Happy New

Year!" Thin laughter greeted this display. Then we stood around waiting to see what I would do with the piece of coal and the bell.

Feeling the surge of panic, I dropped the coal and the bell, grabbed a girl and kissed her. I heard a mass hissing of indrawn breath, and abruptly everybody was kissing everybody, decorously and with proper absence of any sign of enjoyment.

From somebody came the first croak of "Auld Lang Syne," and I had to let go of the girl I had. If there's anything I hate it's being part of that daisy chain of hands and bleating about old acquaintance with a lot of people I've just met and am unlikely to see again.

There was a distinct feeling of relief when we broke off from "Auld Lang Syne," but nobody seemed to know where we should go from there. Some of the guests looked at me as though I should go out and bring in some more coal. I was darned if I was going to play navvy all night. So I said:

"Let's play Iceman's Knock!"

"What is Iceman's Knock?" a lady asked.

"It's like Postman's Knock," I said, "only you go into the kitchen."

Through the stunned silence I saw the lieutenant-colonel gathering himself for the spring into another breach.

"Say, that's jolly good," he said, with a brittle chuckle.

That's about when I went home.

I wonder what sort of a year this will be?